What People Are Saying About *Overcoming The Impostor*

"I know from firsthand experience that being an entrepreneur and growing a business is difficult. *Overcoming The Impostor* should be required reading for every entrepreneur who wants to buck the odds and achieve success. It can be done, and Kris explains how to do it."

—David F. Jones, president and CEO,
EnableComp || Complete Holdings Group

"Kris Kelso has discovered the keys to fighting off your own worst enemy—the critical voice inside your head. Every entrepreneur should read this book."

—Dr. Tom Hill, author of *Living at the Summit*
and *Chicken Soup for the Entrepreneur's Soul*

"'Community is where you gain perspective—where you realize that the problems and challenges you are facing are the same challenges that many others have faced (and beaten) before you and that many are facing alongside you today.'

This excerpt from *Overcoming The Impostor* speaks perfectly to what you will find reading this book: a community of people who have all struggled with the feeling that they don't belong, like their friends or colleagues are going to discover they're a fraud, and that they don't actually deserve your title, job, or accomplishments. Kris is an authentic entrepreneur and author who's not afraid to share his own experiences around this vulnerable topic. This book reminded me that we all feel like this at some point. Most importantly, *Overcoming The Impostor* gave me practical advice and confidence that I can apply to tell those little voices in my head to shut up. A fantastic and quick read that will have a lasting impact on your personal and professional life."

—Jessica Harthcock, CEO and
co-founder, Utilize Health

"*Overcoming The Impostor* is an excellent read. For entrepreneurs, you can learn to work or work to learn. Don't let the demons of The Impostor keep you from your rightful place as a leader and soothsayer of ideas. This book will allow you to turn your inner impostor voice into a voice of reason. Looking deep into that space we all fear is the real evidence of growth as a person and valued member of the community. Ultimately, you will be able to redefine *your* success and find the right path for you."

—J. Tod Fetherling, CEO, Perception Health

"I am an entrepreneur and have had the privilege of working with hundreds of people. Entrepreneurs must be what Kris calls Explorers, who 'aren't concerned with having all the answers; they're focused on finding the answers.' Also, Kris points out the importance of mentorship and helps you understand the power of failure as a teacher on the road to success."

—Julia Polk, founder and chief strategy officer, Decode Health

"In *Overcoming The Impostor*, Kris Kelso pulls back the curtain on an entire generation of executives, entrepreneurs, and seemingly successful people who see themselves as impostors and who fear being exposed. With killer clarity, he identifies the symptoms and consequences of living with impostor syndrome and is generous with tried and true strategies to not only combat the inner critic, but to actually use it to your advantage. A must read for any business leader!"

—Hunter Atkins, chairman, Synovus Bank Nashville

OVERCOMING THE IMPOSTOR

OVERCOMING THE IMPOSTOR

SILENCE YOUR INNER CRITIC AND LEAD WITH CONFIDENCE

KRIS KELSO

DEXTERITY
NASHVILLE

DEXTERITY

Dexterity, LLC
604 Magnolia Lane
Nashville, TN 37211

Printed in the United States of America.

First edition: 2021
10 9 8 7 6 5 4 3 2 1

ISBN: 978-1-947297-23-4 (trade paper)
ISBN: 978-1-947297-24-1 (eBook)

Publisher's Cataloging-in-Publication data

Names: Kelso, Kris, author.
Title: Overcoming the impostor : silence your inner critic and lead with confidence / Kris Kelso.
Description: Includes bibliographical references. | Nashville, TN: Dexterity, 2021.
Identifiers: ISBN 978-1-947297-23-4 (pbk.) | 978-1-947297-24-1 (ebook)
Subjects: LCSH Impostor phenomenon. | Fear of failure. | Leadership. | Entrepreneurship. | Success. | Success in business. | Self-actualization (Psychology) | BISAC BUSINESS & ECONOMICS / Leadership | BUSINESS & ECONOMICS / Entrepreneurship | SELF-HELP / Personal Growth / Success
Classification: LCC BF637.I46 .K45 2021 | DDC 158.1--dc23

Book design by PerfecType, Nashville, TN.
Cover design by Gore Studios Inc.

To Mary, for always believing I would overcome The Impostor.

CONTENTS

INTRODUCTION

One of my inner struggles in my early years as an entrepreneur was never quite identifying with the passion that I saw in other entrepreneurs. I would hear them say things like this:

"I was compelled to start this business and to solve this problem."

"I think about this problem every waking moment."

"I would work on this even if there were no money to be made; it's a mission."

I never really felt that strongly about the businesses of which I've been a part. Sure, there were things that interested me and things that excited me, but I've always been able to turn it off on the weekend or focus on other interests at the same time.

But a few years ago, when I began to talk about my battle with The Impostor, my term for what's known as impostor syndrome (which I'll define more clearly in the book)—both to large groups as well as one-on-one to my clients and other entrepreneurs—the responses I heard told me that this was a widely shared and significant challenge. People came to me after a speech and said, "You changed my life today." The more I studied, the more I spoke, and the more I listened, the more a fire began to grow.

And suddenly, I understood that passion. I had a mission—a calling. This was a problem I felt compelled to solve. I would talk about this even if there were no profit in it for me.

I've been told for years that I should write a book. I even started writing a different one nearly ten years ago. I wrote about a quarter of it and threw it away. I doubt that anyone would have wanted to read it. I didn't even want to read it. It was pretty dull because I was writing just to do it. There was no passion—just a desire to get it done—and it showed.

But this book—this one had to be written. I didn't have a choice.

That doesn't mean it came easy. It took me two years to really get started. Early on, I told many of the people around me that I was going to write a book, just for the accountability. I thought that if people were asking me about it, I'd be motivated to get it done. But that wasn't enough. After a year or so of little progress, I stopped talking about it quite so much.

During that time, I studied, I continued to speak, and I listened to other entrepreneurs and leaders describe their experiences. All the while, I battled the feeling that I wasn't qualified to write this book or that I didn't have what it took to make it great.

Even when I finally made some progress, there were moments when I'd hit a wall and just need to walk away from it for a week or two. I even had to use some of my own tricks—some of the tips and tools I'm about to share with you—to push beyond my doubts and do more than I felt I was capable of doing.

It's Not Just for Entrepreneurs

I'm an entrepreneur, and many of the stories in this book are about entrepreneurship. But even if you're not an entrepreneur (or perhaps you are one but don't *feel* like one), you'll see how changing your thinking and battling the voice inside your head that wants to hold you back will open a world of possibilities for you.

Entrepreneurial leadership takes many forms, from the founder of a technology start-up to the owner of a home-based business or a pastor who is planting a new church. Many artists, musicians, doctors, and tradespeople are entrepreneurs by default. Even inside large companies, there are people who are leading new initiatives with an entrepreneurial approach, breaking new ground and learning as they go.

We're *all* entrepreneurs at some level. Gone are the days when people worked for a single company for forty years and then retired, and then that company took care of them for the rest of their lives. Each of us is managing our own life and career and having to decide when to take risks and when to step back or step aside.

This book isn't just about my entrepreneurial journey, though. I've compiled many different stories from people in different walks of life and a wide range of business situations. My research and the work that I've done have taught me that although this problem is widespread, it's also individual and personalized.

My hope for you is that as you read this book, you'll recognize the times that The Impostor has been at work in your life and career. You'll learn to be more aware when it shows up in the future and ready to deal with it.

These pages are full of the tools and techniques you can use to disarm that inner critic so that you can jump into opportunities more easily and step forward when you want to step back. You'll gain a better understanding of the important roles of community and vulnerability and get a new perspective on failure and success.

I hope this book will give you confidence, but not just a confident feeling. Confidence in your knowledge and understanding of the battle that plays out in your own head. Confidence that it's a battle you can win.

I also hope that you will have a new ability to recognize The Impostor at work in others and to help them win their battle as well. You can become a person who changes someone's life in one conversation. I have seen it happen now more times than I can count.

I look forward to hearing how it happens for you.

ONE

This Is Personal

Did he just call me the "expert"?

I sat there, hoping and praying that no one would ask the question, "What makes you an expert?" I was worried that someone would question my experience or ask me to tell them about other clients I had worked with and similar problems I had solved.

It was day three of my first consulting gig. My former boss, John Levy, had taken a job as a chief information officer and inherited a struggling information technology department. I had recently formed a company, with plans to leave my job and strike out as a consultant, so he agreed to contract me to work on some projects.

Communication in the IT department was weak and dysfunctional. The company relied on custom software to serve its customers, and that software was in constant need of repair. But software issues were being handled in a haphazard, inconsistent way. The business was suffering from the software issues, and trust in the IT department was low.

Though I had no formal training in process improvement, I had always paid attention to breakdowns in process and communication. My former boss, John, knew this, and he believed I could make a big impact, so he assigned the problem to me.

Two days later, I sat in a meeting with the entire software development team. The manager of the group introduced me by saying, "You all know we've had some breakdowns in communication, so that's why we've brought in an expert."

I hadn't proclaimed myself the expert; that title was given to me by someone making an assumption. But I knew I couldn't say, "Actually, I've never done this before, so I'm just going to figure it out."

Yet, that's exactly what I was going to do.

"Figure It Out" Is Part of My Job Description

Most of my career had been defined by figure-it-out moments. Going back to the age of twenty-one, after a few years in the music industry, I took a job at a small business owned by Mike Wharton, a man I knew from church. I was mostly doing manual labor—moving inventory in and out of the warehouse, making deliveries, and so on—but I took an interest in the computers that ran the printing equipment, and Mike noticed.

One day, Mike came to me and asked, "Do you know anything about building a website?" This was in the late 1990s, the age when everyone had a stack of America Online CD-ROMs they'd received in the mail. Websites were somewhat new, and not many small businesses had one.

"Not a thing," I said. I genuinely thought that building a website was way over my head.

"Well, I think we need a website, and I think you're the guy to figure that out, so that's your new job," Mike replied.

Uh, what?

I started asking around, and the initial advice I got was to buy some software that would do a lot of the hard work for me, eliminating the need to write the actual code, known as HTML. But for whatever reason, that didn't sit well with me.

If I was going to do this, I wanted to really understand how it worked. So instead, I bought a book on HTML and read it cover to cover. It made absolutely no sense to me, so I read it again. And a third time.

About the third or fourth time through it, something started to click, and I sat down at a computer and started to experiment. It took a little while, but I figured out how it actually worked, and I started writing.

I built that first website completely from scratch, without using any "helper tools" to write the code for me. It wasn't amazing, but it worked, and I had learned a lot in the process.

A few weeks later, one of our customers called Mike and asked, "Who built your website?"

"Kris did it," he said, "and he can build you one too. Here, talk to him."

Mike not only encouraged me to do more of that kind of work, but he let me do the work on the side and get paid directly, rather than running it through his company. Pretty soon, I had built a handful of websites and made a little extra money.

Not long after that, I was hired by a health care company as an internal website designer, and eventually, I became a programmer. It was an incredible time of learning and growth. After eight years there, I was managing a team of software developers.

Entrepreneurship Kind of Snuck Up on Me

For a long time, I said I never wanted to own a business. I wasn't interested in the headaches, the risk, and the hassle of dealing with employees, taxes, and so on. I had seen members of my family start businesses and struggle, and I didn't want to go down that road.

And then I woke up one morning, and it was as if everything had changed. Suddenly, the only thing that made sense to me was to start my own business. I'm not sure what triggered it, but looking back, I realize that I always had entrepreneurial tendencies; I just hadn't seen them that way. Years later, my wife even told me that she always knew I would own my own business some day.

With no formal education or business experience, I knew there was a lot I didn't know. At that time, there were not the wide range of programs for aspiring entrepreneurs that exist today—at least, none that I knew about.

I can still remember going to a bookstore and buying a stack of books covering all the things I thought I needed to learn: how to set up a consulting engagement, business finance and taxes, how to write a legal contract, and so forth. I took them home and read them all. I found a small business CPA who helped me set up my business entity and gave me a few pointers on using QuickBooks®, and I was off and running.

It was great timing to have a former boss who had just started a new job as a CIO and needed some help.

That first consulting engagement went fairly well. Within a couple of weeks, I had designed a workflow for information to travel through the department, and within a couple of months, we had everyone using it. The company renewed my contract and had me manage an important IT project. And then another.

When those projects went well, John came to me with an even bigger project.

The company was moving to a new building, and he wanted me to manage all of the technology aspects of the build-out and the move. This would include designing and building out a new data center, with new power and cooling equipment, an entirely new network, and the wiring for eighty thousand square feet of office space.

Since I knew John well, I was quite frank with him. "You know I've never done anything like this in my life. I have no experience building a data center or redesigning a network. This is a really complex project."

"Yes, I do," he replied, "but I believe you're the guy to lead it."

I was both excited and terrified. The learning opportunity and experience this project offered were incredible, but the stakes were high if it did not go well. I was in a position to be the fall guy if things went badly.

Fortunately, I was surrounded by some smart and talented people on the project team. We hit our share of bumps in the road, but overall, the project was a great success, and I learned so much in the process.

Over the next few years, I took on many new projects with little experience. It seemed everything I did, I was doing for the first time and learning as I went. All along the way, I was being introduced to people as the expert and being paid well. In truth, I loved the novelty of doing new things and the learning that came with each one. It was such an exciting and fun time in my career.

After several successful projects on my own, I hired a few additional consultants, and before long, I had a team of people running multiple projects across several different clients. Eventually, I took myself out of the labor pool and focused primarily on running the company, finding new clients, and occasionally adding new consultants to the team.

Beginning to Recognize the Voice of The Impostor

Throughout those first few years as an entrepreneur, there was a quiet, but persistent, nagging voice in my head. It said things like,

> "You don't actually know what you're doing; you just know how to sound like you know what you're doing."
>
> "These people think you're an expert, but you're just making this stuff up as you go."
>
> "You are the only person who doesn't deserve to be sitting at this table."
>
> "You didn't create a real business; you're just a guy doing some consulting."
>
> "You would never have landed that first client if it weren't for your former boss hiring you."

Over time, as my business grew, the voice in my head would change tactics:

> "Your business is not a *real* business until you have employees."
> "Your business isn't a *real* business until you have a physical office."
> "Your business isn't a *real* business until you get to $1 million in revenue."
> "Your business isn't a *real* business until you have a management team."
> "You're not *really* a CEO if you gave yourself that title."

Sometimes I could ignore the voice. Sometimes I could rationalize away the voice. But it would always come back with something new—some new reason that I wasn't who I claimed to be or who everyone around me seemed to think I was.

For a while, I thought I was the only one who had that voice inside my head. I battled it as best I could, but often felt like I was pulling the wool over people's eyes. I had an underlying fear that sooner or later someone was going to figure out that I was just making this all up as I went and that I didn't really have the depth of experience everyone seemed to assume I had.

Someone was bound to figure out that my success was just a string of lucky breaks, that I'd only been successful because I'd hired a lot of people who were smarter and more experienced than I was or that I'd gotten many of my clients through referrals and relationships rather than having a real sales process.

It was many years later, in a conversation with an executive coach, that I learned about impostor syndrome. Here's a definition from Wikipedia:

> Impostor syndrome (also known as impostor phenomenon, fraud syndrome or the impostor experience) is a psychological pattern in which people doubt their accomplishments and have a persistent, often internalized fear of being exposed as a "fraud." The term was coined in 1978 by clinical psychologists Pauline R. Clance and Suzanne A. Imes. Despite external evidence of their competence, those exhibiting the syndrome remain convinced that they are frauds and do not deserve the success they have achieved. Proof of success is dismissed as luck, timing, or as a result of deceiving others

into thinking they are more intelligent and competent than they believe themselves to be.[1]

Looking back, I realize how often I have been plagued by impostor syndrome. I would look at other entrepreneurs and believe that they were successful because they were educated and talented and had a deep understanding of business and people. But not me. My success was due to a lot of lucky breaks and winging it just long enough to figure some things out.

I would be around other entrepreneurs, and although they treated me like one of their own, I didn't feel like I belonged. I suspected they were just being nice, the way a group of football players lets a little kid run with the ball and everyone pretends to be unable to tackle him.

A few years into my consulting business, I was helping one of my clients recruit and hire a new CIO. As we were talking about qualifications and criteria, the CFO said, "We have to look at their degree, because a degree is the only way you can really know that someone is qualified."

He had no idea that I, the consultant he had hired to help with this replacement, did not have a college degree. I've never taken a single college course. I was afraid of what might happen if he found out. So, I didn't say anything; I just let him talk.

My lack of a college education was a frequent source of insecurity. I imagined that there would come a day when someone would mention some basic business concept—something that everyone learned on the first day of business school, but that I'd never heard. Everyone around the room would smile and nod in agreement, and then they'd all look at me and ask for my thoughts.

Within seconds it would become clear that I had no idea what they were talking about, and they would all be mortified! I would immediately be shunned by the business community, and then some guys in black suits and sunglasses would pull me aside and say, "Sir, you're no longer legally allowed to call yourself an entrepreneur. Please go get a real education, and then maybe we'll let you come back and re-apply for the position."

What I Learned from *G.I. Joe*

Like many kids of my generation, I watched cartoons on Saturday mornings when I was growing up. There was no such thing as on-demand TV in those days, so you had to watch shows when they were being broadcast, and Saturday morning was where the action was.

One of those cartoons was *G.I. Joe*, which always wrapped up with a little mini-cartoon that taught some kind of lesson. Those mini-cartoons always ended the same way: The hero would look at the kids and say, "Now, you know. And knowing is half the battle."

Simply learning that impostor syndrome was a thing—that psychologists recognized it and understood it, and that it happened to a lot of people—was a big relief. It instantly gave me a boost of confidence to know that (a) much of what I was hearing from The Impostor was just a mind game, and (b) I wasn't the only one feeling that way.

But that was, as they say, only half the battle. Recognizing it was a big help, but it took several years to truly understand what was behind it and how to successfully combat it. I hope that by sharing my story, and many others' stories, I can help you learn in a few hours what it took me years to understand.

Hindsight Is 20/20

My career has been defined by figure-it-out moments—those times when I had to learn something quickly and put it into action. I used to see that as a weakness, feeling like I was unprepared or ill-equipped. I've come to realize that it's not a weakness; it's a strength. The ability to figure things out on the fly is a valuable skill.

I've also had strong influences, like Mike and John, who pushed me to do new things and showed confidence in me, even when I wasn't confident in myself. I would feel like I was faking it—that my lack of experience made me a fraud—but I wasn't. I was learning and growing.

> The moments when I was least confident were often the most pivotal moments of my career.

Looking back, I realize that the moments when I was least confident were often the most pivotal moments of my career. I couldn't see it then, but I know now that the feeling of being an impostor is both a dangerous trap *and* a sign of great opportunities ahead.

I also realize that so many people around me—even some of the people I admired and some of the people who intimidated me—have had to deal with those same feelings. The Impostor is like a shadow; everybody has one when the conditions are right, but yours is going to look different than mine.

Things to Consider

Before moving on, take a few minutes to think about and answer these questions:

- Impostor syndrome is an internal struggle—a fear that people see you as something you're not and that you're at risk of being exposed as a fraud. In what kinds of situations do you feel like you aren't who people think you are? Are those feelings justified, or is it all in your head?
- I was fortunate to have several people who saw things in me that I didn't see. Have there ever been people in your life who believed in you

more than you believed in yourself? Did you trust them, or did you resist their efforts to push you out of your comfort zone? How did that turn out?

- Think of a situation in which you had to "figure it out" on the fly. How did you feel? What was the outcome? How was that different (whether good or bad) from the situations where you are comfortable and confident?
- Looking back, has there ever been a time that you felt insecure but that you now view as a pivotal moment in your life or career? What was it? What did you learn?

TWO

It's Like Your Shadow

Peter is the chairman of one large company and is an investor in several others, ranging across industries from construction to restaurants. He's well-connected and well-respected in his community. In the second half of his career, he's been generous with his time and expertise to help other entrepreneurs and business leaders.

For several years, he served as the chairman of a national nonprofit and did a lot of work to raise money for the organization. The nonprofit decided to hold an event to honor him alongside another supporter, who was a senior leader at one of the nation's largest companies.

"Don't give me this award," he told them. "Just honor that guy, and leave me out of it."

When I asked Peter why he didn't want to receive the award, his answer surprised me. "That other guy," he said, "he's so well connected, he can make three phone calls and raise a half a million dollars. I've helped raise some money for this organization, but I don't have near the level of influence he has. I would feel like I was being given a token award next to him."

I responded, "What if he feels exactly the opposite? It could be that he's looking at you and feeling like he doesn't deserve the award because all he did was make a few phone calls, while you've served and led and influenced."

Peter's expression told me he had never considered that thought. The very thing that he saw as a weakness—having to work hard to raise support—might be viewed as a strength to someone who didn't have to work nearly as hard.

It's Just An Illusion

Some people refer to that voice as the inner critic or the voice of the saboteur. I've begun simply referring to that voice as The Impostor, both because it's trying to convince me that *I* am an impostor and to remind myself that the voice *itself* is not real; it's just a psychological trap.

The Impostor is like a shadow. We've all got one when the conditions are right, and each of ours is unique to us, but it's not a real thing.

There's no such thing as darkness; there's only light or the absence of light. *Darkness* is just a word to describe the absence of light. There's no such thing as cold; there's only heat or a lack of heat. *Cold* is just a word to describe the absence of heat.

A shadow is not actually a real thing; it's just a space where the light doesn't shine quite as bright as the surroundings.

The Impostor is the same way. That voice inside my head that has told me all those things about my business not being real and that I don't know what I'm doing is not real; it's just a lack of confidence that looks and sounds an awful lot like me.

The Impostor Doesn't Play Favorites

The psychologists who defined impostor syndrome originally thought that it primarily affected professional women. In the 1970s, when the first research was conducted, it was focused on women who were competing in the "man's world" of corporate America and how they felt like frauds despite their obvious records of success and achievement.

It wasn't long, though, before further research showed that—wait for it—men can be insecure, too! What a shock, right? Today we understand that impostor syndrome is not a women's problem; it's a human problem. Though women are more likely than men to *acknowledge* those feelings, multiple studies have shown that men and women share the experience equally[2]; women are just more honest about it.

It affects more people than you might think. Some studies show that up to 70 percent of the population will deal with feelings of being a fraud at some point in their lives.[3] For some, it's situational, while others carry that feeling into nearly everything they do.

Impostor Syndrome Is More Prevalent Among High Achievers

Many people are surprised to learn that impostor syndrome tends to be more prevalent among high achievers—people who are ambitious and competitive and who push the boundaries; people who are not satisfied with coasting through life; people who take risks and try new things. These people are more likely to wrestle with The Impostor.

You might think it would be the other way around, that the more ambitious and driven you are, the less likely you are to feel like a fraud. But the opposite is true. Unambitious people don't struggle as much with feeling like a fraud because they simply don't care. They're not trying to improve; they're fine with coasting through life and keeping things the way they are. There's no reason to feel like a fraud if they do the same thing day in and day out for their entire lives.

Author Maya Angelou once said, "I have written eleven books, but each time I think, *Uh oh, they're going to find out now. I've run a game on everybody, and they're going to find me out.*"

Before becoming cohost of the wildly popular show *Mythbusters*, Adam Savage landed his dream job, working for Industrial Light and Magic in 1998. Despite all his qualifications, there wasn't a week that went by that he didn't think someone was going to tap him on the shoulder and tell him it was time to leave.

"Everybody in a creative field feels that way at times," he said.[4]

The greater—and in particular, the more visible—your success, the more likely you are to feel like you've pulled off a great charade. At some point along the way, you've probably been in over your head or unsure of the next steps, but managed to figure it out.

It's Nearly Universal Among Entrepreneurs

I could not find a study that specifically targeted entrepreneurs, but in my experience working with hundreds of entrepreneurs, I have found impostor syndrome to be the one challenge that is nearly universal among them. Most of what has been written about impostor syndrome has focused on women in male-dominated environments or on young people coming out of college and entering the workforce. Not a lot has been written about the prevalence of The Impostor among successful, courageous, risk-taking people.

But it's true. Many successful entrepreneurs have struggled with self-doubt and had moments when they weren't sure that they actually knew what they were doing. Here are a few reasons that entrepreneurs, as a group, are one of the most likely to experience impostor syndrome.

They're Breaking New Ground

Entrepreneurs, by definition, are often in the position of trying things for the first time and figuring them out along the way. They create things that didn't exist before, or they take old, established products and systems and turn them on their heads.

This leads to a lot of trial and error and a lot of failures and mistakes. Every successful entrepreneur has a long list of failed experiments—some huge and others small—in his or her past. It can be easy to feel like the failures define an entrepreneur, while the successes (which are usually fewer and farther between) may just be the result of luck.

A few years into my first business, I thought of a "brilliant" new way that we could work with our clients. I was so confident that it would be a success that I hired a marketing firm to help us put together materials and presentations. We worked for months to get ready to unveil this great new idea to the world.

We signed up exactly one client, who paid us only a little more than we spent on marketing. Not exactly a home run. Though my business was a success overall, there were plenty of mistakes like that along the way.

They're Almost Constantly in Sales Mode

Entrepreneurship involves a lot of selling. The most obvious sales job is selling products or services to potential customers. In the early phases of a business, entrepreneurs may be the only salespeople in the company. They might be selling a product that isn't yet as high quality as desired or a service that is not completely defined and tested.

But that might be the easiest sale entrepreneurs have to make. They also have to sell a vision of the future, of what they're setting out to build, and of possibilities that haven't yet been realized.

Entrepreneurs have to sell their ideas to potential employees who they want to come join their company. They have to convince people to come alongside them, sometimes working crazy hours for little pay and sparse benefits, and to believe that the rewards on the other side of success will be worth the sacrifices.

A small percentage of entrepreneurs will raise money from investors, which is essentially selling a stake in the company's future for cash right now. Selling investors is one of the hardest sales jobs I've ever had to do. The ratio of nos to yeses is usually at least 99 to 1.

If you've ever led a young company, you know that the problem with all that selling is that you're always presenting the best version of yourself, your team, your idea, and your business. You are highlighting all the positives, while you know deep down there are plenty of negatives as well. You know there are cracks and flaws in the plan. You know there are things you haven't figured out yet, and there are assumptions you have made that you can't yet prove.

They're Put on a Pedestal

Entrepreneurship has become in vogue in our society, and entrepreneurs are sometimes celebrated as superheroes.

A CEO named Toby Thomas used an illustration that has become my go-to description of entrepreneurship: a man riding on a lion.

People look at the man on the lion and think, "This guy's really got it together. He's so brave!" And all the while, the man riding the lion is thinking, "How in the world did I get on this lion, and how do I keep from getting eaten?"[5]

The imagery here is remarkably accurate. I cannot count the number of times I've been given accolades, admiration, and verbal high-fives for the risks I've taken and the things I've accomplished as an entrepreneur. Yet on the inside, I'm not celebrating; I'm usually freaking out a little bit. What looks to others like strength and boldness feels to me like a series of near-catastrophes.

Entrepreneurs are celebrated for being the risk-takers they are, but that celebration often feels undeserved. It feels fraudulent.

That combination—having a close relationship with uncertainty, being continually in sales mode, and being glorified by others—puts entrepreneurs on a crash course with The Impostor. It provides plenty of material for The Impostor to work with, plenty of options to convince you that you're not really who everyone seems to think you are.

You Are Likely a Target

Tyrone had been a software developer for nearly ten years when he and a couple of coworkers decided to start their own company. He relied on several relationships to find his first couple of clients, and since they did good work, their business grew mostly through referrals and word of mouth.

It took many years, though, for Tyrone to think of himself as an entrepreneur. He knew there was a lot that he didn't know about running a company, and so his success as a business owner never quite felt real, even when he had more than a dozen employees.

Even if you aren't an entrepreneur in the traditional sense, the fact that you are reading this book means that you're the type of person who wants to learn and grow. You're interested in improving yourself, and with that pursuit comes a level of risk-taking and uncertainty.

At some point, if you haven't already, you are likely to face The Impostor. But if you're looking for the same struggles and insecurities that I faced, you're going to be caught by surprise. The Impostor won't attack you in the same way it attacked me. Everyone gets their own *customized* Impostor, and you will need to learn to recognize the tactics The Impostor will try to use on you.

Things to Consider

Before moving on, take a few minutes to think about and answer these questions.

- People who are battling The Impostor have a hard time accepting compliments and recognition at face value. Can you think of a time when you were being praised by others, but you felt undeserving? Looking back, who was right?
- Entrepreneurs (and many other kinds of people) spend a lot of time in sales mode, presenting only the best version of themselves and their work. How often are you in that mode? How often are you able to turn that off and just be real? Which situation is more comfortable? Which is more productive?
- Many of the people we admire and respect have also had to face The Impostor at times. Who is a person you consider to be successful? How likely is it that they have felt like an impostor at some point in their career? If you knew that they had struggled with impostor syndrome, would that change your view of their success?

THREE

Your Own Customized Impostor

Rusty is the CEO of a company that distributes supplies to independent hardware stores. Over a fifteen-year period, he has guided the company through multiple recessions, customer turnover, the loss of key staff members to competitors, and many other challenges that small businesses face. Through it all, the company has continued to be profitable and treated their employees well.

And yet, he still struggles with the idea that he's not a real CEO, for one simple reason: His father started the company.

Rusty went to law school, but he quickly found that he didn't enjoy being an attorney. He was working in sales at another company when his father asked him to come work for the family business. He was reluctant—he didn't want to simply follow in his father's footsteps—but ultimately, he accepted.

He spent several years working in different areas of the business, learning the ropes. Eventually, he was the second in command, and not long afterward, his father was finally able to retire, leaving Rusty in charge.

Fifteen years later, Rusty still struggled with the idea that he was not a legitimate CEO. "I just feel like the guys in the warehouse are looking at me, thinking, *He's only there because his dad gave him the job*." Maybe some of them were. They almost certainly thought that in the first few years, but even fifteen years later?

I told him, "Rusty, if you were going to flush this company down the toilet, you would have done it long before now."

The Impostor Comes Tailor Fit to You

The Impostor attacks people in unique ways; you will experience it differently than I did. For me, education (or the lack of it) was a recurring theme. I don't have a college degree, and I struggled for many years with feeling inferior because of that.

But education might not be your insecurity. It wasn't Rusty's.

The Impostor will construct a specific and personal rationale for why *you* are a fraud. It might be about your family background or where you grew up. It could be a lack of experience or of a particular kind of experience. Maybe it's a struggle with perfectionism, never feeling like you can quite get anything right.

Perhaps there's an award you wish you could win that serves as a seal of approval in your mind, but you've never quite achieved it. Maybe it's about fame, notoriety, or the number of followers you have.

It knows your buttons and triggers and will use them against you.

Tom has written several books and contributed to major magazines and websites. It seems like whenever he meets new people and they hear he's a writer, they immediately tell him about their book idea. It gets old, but he is polite about it. When he's struggling, though, The Impostor will bring this up, and tell him that he's nothing special, because *everyone* has ideas for a book. Never mind that writing is hard work and he's made a good living at it for years. All he hears is that he's no more talented than the average person.

Julie is a high school principal and sits on a school board with several local business leaders. Even though she runs an organization of several thousand people (students, faculty, and support staff), she feels inferior because she doesn't have the same title and doesn't earn the same money as the other members. The Impostor tells her that her leadership and administrative skills don't really count because she deals mostly with kids.

It's so individual and personal that the very thing that haunts one person may be the opposite of what haunts someone else. On the next page are some examples of triggers I've heard from different people. Notice the contrast.

I know one business owner who has dozens of employees and has built out a management team that handles most of the day-to-day work. Yet she doesn't feel like a real CEO because she started her business and gave herself that title by default.

Just down the street, another business owner doesn't feel like a real entrepreneur because he

One Person's Weakness Is Another Person's Crutch

I don't have a college degree; I'm just figuring this out or making this up.	People assume that I have all the answers because of my degree, but I'm just figuring this out along the way.
I'm not well-connected like these other people.	I'm only here because of my connections and relationships; I couldn't make it without them.
I come from a poor family; I don't have the same means as my peers.	I've only made it because of my wealthy family; I haven't actually proven myself.
I'm in this alone; no one would want to partner with me.	I have a great team; there's no way I could make it on my own.
I'm just an idea person; I have to rely on others to get things done.	I'm not really that smart; I'm just getting by on hard work.

didn't start his company from scratch; he purchased it from the previous owner despite the fact that he's completely revamped the business model, turned the operation around, and is seeing record profits.

No matter what you've accomplished, there will always be holes that The Impostor can exploit to try to convince you that your success is not real. But those holes are not flaws; they're just the unique aspects of your story that make it different from everyone else's.

How to Recognize the Tactics of The Impostor

Jamie was the youngest of five siblings, and growing up, she always had a lot of people around to "help" her. Even when she was just playing with her toys, if she struggled at all, it seemed like someone would always jump in and take care of it for her.

Over time, and without even realizing it, she developed an internal belief that she couldn't ever do anything on her own. The Impostor would tell her that she needed to find someone, not just to help, but to do it for her so that it would be done right.

Years later, as an entrepreneur, she still struggled with the idea that she wasn't up to the task, no matter what the task might have been. She had great ideas but never felt confident moving forward unless she could find someone else to take the lead and show her how to do it. Only once she recognized this tactic of The Impostor was she able to get over that false limitation and build a great business of her own.

The Impostor knows your history. It uses your voice and will make use of your vocabulary. It's in your own head, so it sounds familiar and comfortable. It would be so much easier to refute if it were the voice of a crazy person, but it's not. It sounds a lot like reason, logic, and prudence.

I'm only being realistic, you think to yourself. *I don't want to get my hopes up. I don't want to set myself up for disappointment*. Each of these is code for, "I don't want to take a risk."

The Impostor is keenly aware of your weaknesses. Maybe you're not a great writer or an eloquent speaker. Perhaps you get nervous in certain situations. Maybe you have a disability or a limitation that you think will hold you back.

The Impostor will weaponize that knowledge and convince you that your flaw is a fatal one. The Impostor tells you that although everyone has weaknesses, *yours* is the one that cannot be overcome or the one that disqualifies people from doing whatever it is that you are setting out to do. The Impostor will even prevent you from seeing that weakness in other people or at least convince you that they aren't nearly as flawed as you are.

The Impostor will make you feel unique and special, but for all the wrong reasons.

It knows how much luck and chance may have played into your journey. (News flash: Every success story includes a healthy dose of luck and chance.) It knows all the cracks and flaws in your plans—the times that you barely made it work and the hundreds of thousands of ways it could have gone terribly wrong.

Everyone's journey has similar flaws, of course. You just can't see them with the same clarity that you can see your own.

The best lies are 90 percent truth. It's easy to spot a blatant lie, but the lies that are mostly true are hard to identify and even harder to refute. We believe these lies because they *mostly* line up with the other things we know to be right.

The Impostor knows all too well how to take the truth and bend and shape it to feed your insecurities. It will use facts and actual events, and season them with assumptions. It will take the words people have said and insert meaning that isn't really there. Even worse, it will take the words people *haven't* said and convince you there are all kinds of reasons behind the silence.

Personalization Keeps You Isolated

You may have tried at times to find common ground with others who have the same voice inside their head, only to be discouraged when they don't experience it in the same way that you do.

Once, after I finished speaking to a large audience, a woman approached me and asked how I prepare for a speech and how I deal with the nerves. I could tell that she was a little disappointed when I told her that I don't usually get very nervous. (I've been speaking in front of audiences since I was a teenager, and I genuinely enjoy it.)

But just because getting on stage in front of people is not my weakness or my area of insecurity, that doesn't mean I don't have any. It also doesn't mean I'm the greatest public speaker! There are many more well-known and talented speakers than I who get nervous every time they take the stage.

Many people have struggled, and continue to struggle, with the feeling of being an impostor in some area of their lives and careers. Just because their struggles are different than yours, that doesn't make them any less real. The battles are individual and personal, but the fight is the same.

Things to Consider

Before moving on, take a few minutes to think about and answer these questions.

- We each have a different perspective, shaped by our culture, upbringing, and experiences. What part of your life and story have you considered a weakness, while others (with a different perspective) might view it as a strength?
- The Impostor puts a magnifying glass on our flaws, making them appear much bigger and more problematic than they really are. What flaw or shortcoming have you allowed The Impostor to magnify? What could you accomplish if you were able to overcome that perceived weakness?

- One event or incident, especially during our formative years in childhood and adolescence, can shape our thinking for the rest of our lives. What belief or habit from your childhood is holding you back? What would be possible if you were to completely change that belief or habit?

FOUR

The Impostor Is More Than a Nuisance

Eric was part of a pioneering entrepreneurial company in the 1990s, when the internet was changing from a research and development network to a system that an average person might use. His ten-person company developed technology that used both telephone lines and satellite links to speed up the transmission of data across the internet.

Their work caught the attention of a multibillion dollar satellite company, who came to see Eric and learn about what his company was doing. To his surprise, a few weeks later, this big company offered him a position as vice president to head up an important new project.

Suddenly, Eric was on the big stage. Before long, he was making monthly flights from Silicon Valley to New York, to personally update the CEO on the project.

Over time, as Eric had success, he was given even more responsibility. Engineering. Vendor relationships. Marketing strategy. He was influencing billion-dollar decisions.

All the while, though, The Impostor was chipping away at his confidence. "This can't be right," it would say. "You don't belong here. You're just a kid from a small town. What were these people thinking, putting you in charge of all this?"

Eventually, his struggle caught up with him. He began to pull back from his work, missing meetings and procrastinating on big assignments. He was running from the fear of failure.

"It became a self-fulfilling prophecy," he said. "I worried that I couldn't measure up, and my performance suffered as a result."

After blowing one of the most important presentations of the year, Eric was fired. He knows it was his own fault. "I approached it wrong. I should have asked for help." He knows that his fear had prevented him from being successful.

"They saw something in me that I couldn't see. I refused to see it. I convinced myself it wasn't there, and eventually, I proved it wasn't there."

Impostor syndrome is more than just a bad feeling. It can negatively affect your life, health, and ability to perform in a number of ways.

The Impostor Will Pile on the Stress

Angela had been a realtor for about three years when she landed the biggest deal of her career: a contract four times as large as any she'd ever done before. You would think that getting that size deal would feel like a validation, but she was completely overwhelmed by the pressure, especially when she realized that the realtor on the other side of the deal was a thirty-year veteran whom she had admired as a rock star in her industry.

The pressure of getting this deal done caused her to make some poor decisions along the way. She over scrutinized every conversation and ended up losing her cool during negotiations. She nearly lost the deal and permanently soured her relationship with the other realtor.

Entrepreneurship comes with a lot of stress. The stakes are high: Your livelihood, and that of your family (and probably many other families), is dependent on the decisions and choices you make every day. Often, the decisions are difficult ones, and the answers aren't nearly as clear-cut as you'd like them to be.

The Impostor can turn a typical decision into a difficult one and make a difficult decision nearly impossible.

But if you add to that stress the persistent fear of failure, or the fear of being exposed as a fraud, it can become overwhelming. The Impostor can turn a typical decision into a difficult one and make a difficult decision nearly impossible.

The Impostor will cause you to rehash conversations and situations in which you are not sure you did the right thing. It will prevent you from feeling confident in a decision you made, not allowing you to put it behind you and move forward.

It will also cause you to rehearse and worry about potential problems you haven't even encountered yet.

It's well documented that mental and emotional stress can take a physical toll. When you worry unnecessarily about the future, you may lose sleep (or sleep poorly), neglect exercise, and eat unhealthily—all of which can affect your ability to perform at your best and think clearly. When you aren't thinking clearly, The Impostor has a playground in your vulnerable mind.

The Impostor Will Burn You Out

Ian was an independent consultant who would bounce around from project to project and from client to client. Though he had some good relationships with other consultants and a few firms in his area, he never felt like he was quite as good as his peers. He especially hated that he couldn't find enough of his own clients and had to rely on other consultants to include him in their projects.

To compensate, he just tried to outwork them. He put in a ton of hours and spent most of his weekends perfecting his presentations and fine-tuning reports.

Eventually, though, he hit a wall. He had been working so much and taking on so much stress that he started having some serious health issues. Burning the candle at both ends caught up to him, and he had to take an extended break.

Two of the symptoms of impostor syndrome are overpreparation and overproduction, both in the interest of proving yourself to measure up to the image you believe others have of you. Though high levels of preparation and production are generally *good* things, they might be more about maintaining your image or overcoming your insecurity than they are about the actual value of what you're producing. In that case, they're unhealthy and probably hurting you more than they're helping you.

Burnout occurs when your stress level reaches the point of mental and emotional exhaustion. It happens slowly, over time, but can end suddenly, when you reach a breaking point. If you allow The Impostor to push you to work harder than necessary, over a prolonged period of time, you could be heading for disaster.

The Impostor Will Slow You Down

Lisa finally found the courage to leave her job and start her own business. She spent a lot of time setting up her office, working on a website, getting business cards, and writing content to post on her blog and share on social media. But she was avoiding one crucial task: going out and talking to potential customers!

> Procrastination is failure avoidance.

She always found a way to feel busy, but she wasn't generating much income. Finally, she realized that the fear of being rejected—of being told that she wasn't good enough—was keeping her from doing the most important thing she needed to do to make her business successful.

Procrastination is failure avoidance. If you allow The Impostor to convince you that you're likely to fail at the most important things you need to do, you may fall into the trap of avoiding those important things.

You may find yourself doing the following things.

- *Avoiding interactions where you feel vulnerable*, including conversations with clients, experts, or other influential people who could help you.
- *Avoiding productive work*, especially if you are not confident in your output.
- *Avoiding "the big dance"*—that great opportunity to get in front of an audience or to present to a whale of a prospect.

A common procrastination trap for entrepreneurs is known as "productive procrastination"—working hard on the things that are easy in order to avoid the things you don't want to do.

Entrepreneurs always have an endless list of things that can be done, so it's easy to make yourself believe you are busy, when you're actually just avoiding something uncomfortable (but important).

The Impostor Will Convince You That You Can't Ask for Help

In an episode of the TV show *The Office*, Jim Halpert is asked by his new boss to deliver a "rundown" of all his clients. The problem is that Jim has no idea what his boss means by a "rundown." He tries all kinds of ways to figure out what his boss means without coming out and asking him directly, but everything his boss says just confuses him more and annoys his boss in the process.

I know how that feels. Years ago, I was working with a group of entrepreneurs who were preparing to pitch their business ideas to investors. There was a lot of talk about getting a "term sheet," which is simply a document that outlines the terms of an investment deal.

At the time, though, I had never seen a term sheet; I had no idea what one looked like. So I went to a friend who was in the process of raising money from some investors, and I asked if I could take a look at his term sheet.

“Productive procrastination”—working hard on the things that are easy in order to avoid the things you don’t want to do.

"There's nothing special about it. It's pretty standard," was all he said. And I couldn't bring myself to tell him that I didn't know what "standard" meant.

When you worry that others may see you as a fraud or a phony, one of the last things you want to do is reach out and ask for help. There may be help readily available, but your pride prevents you from asking for it, so you continue to struggle in silence. You hurt yourself in multiple ways:

- In your desire to appear as an expert, you miss the opportunity to learn from the experts, which is what helps you to become one.
- By not asking for help, you miss out on building valuable relationships.
- If people see you willingly struggle when help is available, it will erode your credibility rather than build it.

The Impostor's Goal Is Self-Sabotage

If you carry a lot of self-doubt, it will show up in your body language, your tone of voice, and the words you use. People will hear it and see it, and it will work against you.

Self-sabotage, however, goes much deeper than that. It's in the decisions you make.

It took me nearly three years to write this book. Multiple times on that journey, I was tempted to just give up. I didn't feel like an author, and I didn't want to produce a book that was poorly written or disorganized.

I know many published authors, some who've sold millions of books. As long as I hadn't written a book myself, I never felt the need to compare my work to theirs. But I knew that once I wrote a book, I'd be part of that group, and I might feel like the little guy. Even worse, they might think of me as just a wannabe.

So I was tempted to not do it. To avoid those potentially negative feelings, I almost walked away from this important work.

The biggest risk that we face when dealing with The Impostor is that we make a decision to prove it right! If I had decided that I shouldn't write because I wasn't an author, that would become the truth. I would never become an author, not because I couldn't *do* it, but because I couldn't *believe* it.

Self-sabotage happens when you believe something negative about yourself so strongly that your brain works to make it true. Without even realizing it, you subconsciously change your behavior to line up with what you believe, even if you don't *want* to believe it.

The Impostor will force you to put limits on your dreams and your imagination. Instead of dreaming about what's possible, you'll only allow yourself to dream about what's probable—the things you know you can easily achieve.

The End Game Is Regret

> *"Twenty years from now you will be more disappointed by the things you didn't do than by the ones you did."*
>
> —Mark Twain

Perhaps the longest-lasting impact The Impostor can have on your life is regret. When you look back on the opportunities you had but were not bold enough to take advantage of, you may live with disappointment that you let your self-doubt get the better of you.

When you're exhausted from the stress of trying to measure up, you're disappointed by the missed opportunities and the times you could have asked for help, and you've suffered from self-sabotage, you will wish you had overcome The Impostor sooner rather than later.

It's Not All Bad News

Eric was eventually recruited by another large company, where he became the youngest vice president in the history of the organization. During his first week on the job, he was giving a presentation to a group of other executives, and one of them interrupted to essentially tell him he didn't know what he was talking about.

Uh-oh, he thought. *Here it goes again*. Those feelings of being in over his head came flooding back. Fortunately, he had a CEO who took him under his wing and began to mentor him. Over time, he learned how to lean in to that discomfort and recognize his new job for the opportunity that it was: an opportunity to stretch himself, to learn, and to grow.

Impostor syndrome is more than just a negative thought or feeling; it can have a real and harmful impact on your life if you let it control you. By watching for these symptoms, you can recognize when The Impostor is at work and you're at risk of giving in to stress, burnout, and self-sabotage.

But there's another side to that story. The presence of The Impostor can actually be a good sign, letting you know that you're exactly where you need to be.

Things to Consider

Before moving on, take a few minutes to think about and answer these questions.

- The Impostor will convince you that you can't ask for help—that it will expose you and your lack of knowledge. Have you ever been afraid to ask for help, for fear of looking foolish or unprepared? What did you do? How did that fear hold you back?
- Procrastination happens for many reasons, but it's especially dangerous when it's a response to fear. What important work have you been putting off because of the fear of failure or rejection? What would you be able to accomplish if you could eliminate that fear?
- Some stress is legitimate, while other stress is internal and self-inflicted. In what situations does stress keep you from doing your best work? Where does that stress originate? Is it external or internal?

FIVE

The Impostor Is the Way

In 2012 a venture capitalist named Vic Gatto invited me to join Jumpstart Foundry as a mentor, where I'd be helping other entrepreneurs in their program. Jumpstart Foundry was then a start-up accelerator (similar to Techstars or Y Combinator). They would select teams of entrepreneurs with a business idea, give them some seed money, and put them through an intensive, fourteen-week program to get their businesses off the ground, with an emphasis on preparing them to pitch their ideas to larger investors. Programs like these are run in entrepreneurial cities all over the country, with some huge companies like Uber, Dropbox, and Airbnb growing out of these programs.

At the time, I had been running a successful consulting business for about five years, but I knew little about investor-backed start-ups. I felt completely in over my head when I went to the first meeting. The room was full of successful entrepreneurs, investors, entrepreneurship professors, and all kinds of industry experts and business leaders.

The first few weeks involved a kind of dating process, where the entrepreneurial teams worked with a lot of different mentors in order to learn about them and what they brought to the table. About week four, the teams began asking specific mentors to join their team for the rest of the program and making an offer of some small amount of equity in their companies as compensation.

Being the impostor that I was, I genuinely thought I was there primarily to learn. I was really curious about the program and about venture-backed start-ups in general, but I didn't think I had a whole lot to offer these entrepreneurs in return. Many of them had MBAs, and some had a great deal of experience in their industry.

I assumed that I'd participate in the first few weeks, would not get asked to join any teams, and then would show up at the end as an observer for the big pitch day event. I'd gain some insight into the start-up world and meet some really smart people, but that would be it.

I was wrong. It wasn't long before I was asked to mentor several of the teams, and I realized that I had a lot to offer. Even though some of the things these entrepreneurs were doing were new to me, there were many ways that my experience was valuable to them.

Although The Impostor can be destructive if you let it overwhelm and control you, its presence can be a good sign. It means you may be on the brink of something great.

Warning: Learning Opportunities Ahead

The Impostor rarely speaks up when you're in your comfort zone. If you're in a routine, doing the same things you've always done, you're unlikely to feel like a fraud. The confidence that comes from easy wins can give you a temporary feeling of victory over The Impostor.

But that's not where growth happens. You rarely learn in your comfort zone. You don't improve by continuing to do what comes easily. Improvement usually involves some level of discomfort.

The Impostor is most active when you're pushing the boundaries—when you're stretching yourself. When you hear The Impostor saying, "You're about to fake something," you should translate that to mean, "You're about to learn something."

When we were children, we learned by doing. We tried, failed, and tried again. Want to learn to walk instead of crawl? Pull yourself up and give it a shot. Fall over? Try again.

It's a natural way to learn, driven by curiosity, hunger, and a dissatisfaction with the status quo. There's more out there—not just more to have, but more to do and more to be.

Then we go to school, and something about the structure of formal education trains us to believe that we learn something first and then go out into the world and do it once we've learned it. Years and years of this convince us by the time we are adults that learning and doing are two separate events, and one precedes the other. But that's not how life actually works.

We learn by doing. We learn by failing. We learn by trying and failing and trying again.

The truth is, I learned a lot during those early years with Jumpstart Foundry. I looked at dozens of different business models and saw a lot of different personalities and teams operating under a great deal of pressure. I learned a lot about the venture capital market and how investors make decisions.

I sat in rooms with marketing experts as they guided a company through a complete rebranding process. I worked alongside financial experts, developing complex financial models and projections. I learned about industries and markets I'd never been exposed to before.

And I was there to mentor.

Education is a lifelong journey, not just an early period in our lives. There are many ways to learn, whether it's reading books, listening to teachers, or watching a demonstration. We also learn by immersion—by diving into a situation where we know very little and can feel overwhelmed and out of place.

If I had declined Vic's offer to join Jumpstart Foundry, out of fear that I would look like a fool or have nothing to offer, I would have missed out on so much learning and so many opportunities that followed.

When The Impostor kicks in and tells you that you're in over your head, that's often a sign of a learning opportunity. Don't run from it—embrace it!

We learn by doing. We learn by failing. We learn by trying and failing and trying again.

You're Surrounded by Smart and Talented People

Successful people put themselves in the company of other successful people. Sometimes it's intentional—actively navigating your way to those you want to know—and other times, it's just a product of success. Doing well will propel you to places where others are also doing well.

Success expert Jim Rohn once said, "You are the average of the five people you spend the most time with." The company you keep will be a significant driver of the direction of your life and career. If you want to improve yourself, you should regularly be in situations where you might feel inferior.

When you hear The Impostor starting to say things like the statements below, that's a *good* sign!

- You don't belong here.
- You're in over your head.
- These people are out of your league.
- You can't keep up.
- You have nothing to offer this group.

It means you're among people who are going to challenge you, grow you, and inspire you to do more and think bigger. You should not be running from those situations; you should see them for the gift that they are and lean in to those opportunities.

Just a couple of years into running my consulting business, I learned about an organization called The Alternative Board (TAB). TAB is a membership organization that puts business owners together to form boards that meet on a regular basis to serve as advisors to one another. I was introduced to the local chapter owner, who invited me to visit a board meeting and consider joining.

At the time, my business was a one-man-show; I hadn't yet hired anyone or grown beyond my own abilities. Sitting around a conference table with a half dozen owners of much larger (relatively speaking) businesses was a bit intimidating, but I knew it was the kind of group I needed to be a part of if I was going to move from solopreneur to building an organization.

Early on, the learning was pretty one-sided for me; I was getting a lot more out of the group than I was contributing. With everything I knew about business having come from a stack of books on my desk and a couple of years of consulting on my own, I didn't have a lot to offer these other owners. I was soaking up everything I could from the issues they presented and the advice they were giving one another.

It wasn't long, though, before I was able to offer helpful advice and unique perspectives. In particular, my technology background was valuable to some of the other owners who were struggling to understand technology and apply it to their businesses. As my knowledge grew, so did my ability to engage in those conversations and be part of the solutions.

During the first year as a member of TAB, we had a conference, and the speaker was a businessman named Tom Hill. He was an engaging speaker with a fascinating story, so I reached out to him afterward to learn more about him.

Tom and I had a few conversations, and he eventually invited me to one of several events he hosted each year. It was an invitation-only conference, and most of the attendees were business owners. I flew to Kansas City for the first event, not quite knowing what to expect.

As I walked into the conference center, I felt so out of place. Some large businesses were represented, and a number of multimillionaires were in the room. At that point, I had a six-figure business with only a couple of employees, and I was sitting with people who had flown in on their private planes.

When I mentioned to another attendee that I felt like I didn't belong there, he immediately called me out. "Why would you say you don't belong here? That's crazy. You belong here as much as anyone else in this room."

As I got to know some of the people, I realized that not only were they great people, but that many of them had stories like mine—stories of starting out, learning along the way, making mistakes, and sometimes even starting over.

Many of us were on the same journey of entrepreneurship; some were just further down the road than others. Once I realized that the difference between where I was and where some of these other owners were was not a challenge to be overcome, but an opportunity to be capitalized, I began to have some really powerful conversations.

There's a famous saying that has been attributed to a lot of different people: If you're the smartest person in the room, you're in the wrong room.

The corollary to that is this: If you think you're the dumbest person in the room, stay there! That's exactly the place you need to be. When The Impostor tells you to get out, that may be the best sign that you're in the right place.

Accomplishment Is on the Horizon

Any worthwhile accomplishment is going to involve friction. There are going to be forces working against you (whether they're adversarial or just natural), challenges to overcome, and obstacles that get in your way.

Sometimes, the biggest obstacle is in your own head. It's The Impostor telling you that you shouldn't even bother because you won't succeed.

But here again, the presence of that voice is a sign that something good is possible.

> *"When was the last time you tried something for the first time?"*
>
> *—Switchfoot, "When Was the Last Time"*

Have you ever thought about the fact that everything you've ever done, you at one point did for the first time? Every single accomplishment in your entire life has been preceded by the same thing: *a lack of experience*.

> Every single accomplishment in your entire life has been preceded by the same thing: *a lack of experience.*

During a particularly challenging time in my career, I was considering shifting my business in a completely new direction and was unsure about whether I could do it successfully. I was working with a coach, Dr. Roger Hall, who he taught me about the difference between self-confidence and self-efficacy.

"Self-confidence," he said, "is largely internal. It's a feeling of being sure of yourself. But like most feelings, it's vulnerable."

It's true—our feelings are so fickle. They're easily manipulated and are even affected by what we eat and whether we've had enough rest or exercise. Feelings come and go, and they're rarely a reflection of the truth about a situation.

"Self-efficacy, on the other hand," Dr. Hall said, "is based on objectively looking at your history—the things you have accomplished in the past—and knowing that you have what it takes to move forward."

He further explained that it wasn't about specifically having done the thing I was about to attempt, but about the other successes and experiences in my life being evidence that I had the ability to succeed.

I thought back to that first consulting job when I was hired by a former boss. He put me in charge of communication, though I had no formal training or real experience leading an effort like that. But he knew from our history together that I would be successful. He knew I had the combination of the skills needed and the desire to learn, even though I did not have that exact experience.

He put his reputation on the line based on his belief in my abilities, but it wasn't just a feeling of confidence. He had seen me take on new challenges, learn on the fly, and develop expertise quickly before, and he knew I could do it again.

I had to be willing to make that same bet on myself.

Careful—Let's Maintain Some Balance

That doesn't mean that there's never a time to feel like a legitimate impostor.

If I walked into a hospital operating room dressed like a doctor, prepared to perform surgery, I would certainly feel like a fraud—as I should! I have no medical training or experience, and despite my ability to learn on the fly and adapt to situations, I have no business performing surgery.

Not only are my chances of success in that situation very low (let's face it, they're probably zero), but the stakes are high. The cost of failure could be someone's life. That's not the right situation for trial and error.

You *should* feel like a fraud if you're being intentionally deceptive or you are violating the law or ignoring standards that are meant to protect people. Those are not the signs of a bold risk-taker; they're signs of a genuine impostor!

Impostor syndrome is about feeling like a fraud despite evidence to the contrary. Just being in the operating room and dressing like a doctor is not evidence that I'm a surgeon.

You should never be dishonest or deceptive about your experience and abilities. It's not OK to lie about credentials or expertise just because you believe you can be successful.

Defeating The Impostor is not about believing you can do anything at any time—that's narcissism. It's about putting aside your feelings of self-doubt and looking at the evidence.

Follow the Signs

Entrepreneur Barbara Corcoran, who built and sold a $66 million real estate company before becoming one of the famous investors on the TV show *Shark Tank*, has talked about self-doubt and the fact that it's a positive sign, not a negative one.

"Thank God you doubt yourself, because the one thing that I have learned that is true of every single person who is exceptional in whatever they are doing is self-doubt. Without it, you become big-headed, arrogant," she said.[6] "The curse of being competent is self-doubt, because competence rides on your own self-doubt. It's the edge of doubt that makes you a performer in anything you do."

Though The Impostor can wreak havoc if you let it take over, the presence of The Impostor is actually a positive sign. It means that you're putting yourself in situations where learning and growth are possible, and you're with people who are going to challenge you to improve.

The key, then, is not to make The Impostor disappear, but to learn how to recognize it, manage it, and use it as a guidepost of great opportunities. You've already learned how to recognize it. Over the next few chapters, I'll show you how to manage it.

Things to Consider

Before moving on, take a few minutes to think about and answer these questions.

- Most great learning opportunities are outside of our comfort zone, where we may feel insecure and uncertain. Think of a situation where you felt in over your head. What did you learn during that time?
- Smart and successful people can make us feel inferior without even trying, and that can cause us to back up when we should be pressing in. Who are the people that intimidate you? How can you spend more time with those people?

- The things we're most proud of usually happen on the back side of stressful situations. Think of some of the greatest accomplishments of your life and career. What did you feel in the weeks and months leading up to those accomplishments: confidence or uncertainty?

SIX

Community + Vulnerability Is the Key

Jada had been running her own business for nearly four years, and it was growing at a steady pace. Though she had learned a lot in that time, she still faced new questions almost daily, and she knew there was plenty that she didn't know. As the sole owner of her company, she often felt isolated and wished that she had someone to talk to who understood how difficult it is to run a small business.

She knew there had to be others like her in her area, so she started researching groups and organizations for entrepreneurs. She was a little surprised to find that there were a lot of options, from networking groups to membership organizations and big annual conferences.

As she dove into these communities and organizations, she was really impressed by some of the people she met. There were a lot of smart and successful entrepreneurs, and some of them had amazing ideas. She was often intimidated by the complex business models or the depth of knowledge that these people seemed to have about their industries.

Her business was a simple one. She began to wonder if it was too simple.

Some of the entrepreneurs she met had raised a lot of money from investors. Others had doubled the size of their companies in months rather than years. Some were running their third or fourth business.

Though she saw the value of spending time with other successful business leaders, she also began to realize how much she still had to learn. She worried that she didn't really fit in with the other entrepreneurs she was meeting. They seemed confident, but she was always questioning herself. They all seemed to be miles ahead of her.

Before long, Jada was distancing herself from other business owners to avoid that feeling of not measuring up. She could have benefitted from those relationships, but the insecurity drove her away. She was back on her own again.

Entrepreneurship Is a Lonely Road

Entrepreneurship, like many forms of leadership, can be isolating and lonely. Even when you're surrounded by employees and have a great team, there is no one else who quite bears the burden of ownership that you do.

You may be the only person who has a majority of your net worth tied up in your business or has put your career on the line for the project you're leading. Others may have to make difficult decisions for their departments but aren't having to balance the needs of all stakeholders, including customers, employees, and investors, in the same way that you are.

When you're weighing tough decisions that don't have any easy answers, when you're trying to figure out how in the world you're going to make next week's payroll, when you're facing the possibility of losing your biggest customer, which will throw all your goals out the window—that stress can be tough to handle alone, and it can wear you out to the point of exhaustion.

This is one of the reasons that professional investors (angel investors, venture capitalists, etc.) rarely invest in single-founder companies. They know that the road is hard, and traveling alone is dangerous.

We guard against that danger, primarily by being part of a community.

Community Is the Door

Entrepreneurship communities have sprung up all over the country over the past couple of decades. There are programs, networking groups, physical and virtual spaces, conferences, and events all designed to help entrepreneurs and independent creatives meet one another and find community.

Community is where you gain perspective—where you realize that the problems and challenges you are facing are the same challenges that many others have faced (and beaten) before you and that many are facing alongside you today.

Community is where you hear the stories—both the good and the bad—and realize what's possible. You see the opportunities and the traps. You learn from others' victories and from their mistakes.

Unfortunately, when it comes to The Impostor, not all communities are helpful.

Entrepreneurship events and networking groups can actually strengthen The Impostor. The problem is that in most of these communities, everyone is putting their best foot forward; they're all presenting the best version of themselves, their work, and their business. As we discussed earlier, entrepreneurs are almost always in sales mode, and this is amplified at entrepreneurship events.

> Community is where you gain perspective.

When you get into a room where everyone is showing their absolute best, it can be easy to feel like you are the only one who has a lot of cracks under the surface. You know all the hidden flaws in your own work but only see the shiny exterior of everyone else's.

The Impostor kicks into high gear:

"You don't belong here; this group is beyond you."
"Everyone sees right through your story; you don't measure up."
"Look at your competition; you don't have a chance."
"They're all so confident, but you are so insecure."
"These people own businesses; you've just got a dream."
"Everyone seems to know what they're doing. If you belonged here, you'd know what you were doing too."

The root of impostor syndrome is the fear of being exposed as a fraud, and these types of events can ratchet up that fear.

Vulnerability Is the Key to Unlock That Door

Several years ago, I met with a young entrepreneur who had founded his company shortly after college and had landed some money from a famous investor. He was mostly telling a great story, but I could tell that there was a lot of stress and anxiety behind his words.

As we talked, I told him about the image of the man riding on the lion. I shared with him some of my own struggles, fears, and self-doubt on my entrepreneurial journey. I really tried to open up and reveal that I wasn't Superman, and he didn't have to pretend to be either.

His eyes began to water, and he said, "This is the first real conversation I've had with anyone about how hard this is." He had been struggling to keep up with all the other false images of confident entrepreneurs that he saw around him.

It's a bit of a paradox, but we encourage people more when we show our weaknesses than when we are the picture of strength. By being vulnerable, I actually extended him a lifeline and offered him hope for his own situation. It was a powerful moment that I've never forgotten.

Since then, I've tried to be more vulnerable—more open and honest about myself and my career. I initially did it out of a desire to be more helpful to

We encourage people more when we show our weaknesses than when we are the picture of strength.

others, but it wasn't long before I realized how much it benefitted me as well.

In one of my first opportunities to speak in front of a group of business leaders, I was telling a story about a trip I took to Africa with a nonprofit organization. As I recounted the impact that the trip had on me, I got choked up. My eyes watered, and my voice wavered. I was a little embarrassed to be showing that much emotion, but I powered through it.

Afterward, I was talking with my executive coach, who had been in the audience. I mentioned that I hate it when I get teary during a story like that, and I wished I could do it without tears.

"Why would you want to do that?" he asked immediately. "That was exactly the point that you connected with the audience. People were moved by your emotion. Don't try to stop that from happening."

Most people respect leaders who are authentic much more than they do those who try to appear perfect. When you acknowledge your weaknesses—your mistakes, fears, and insecurities—you actually build trust with those around you. They believe you more and give more credibility to your thoughts and ideas.

Being vulnerable also helps you combat The Impostor. When you're covering up your weaknesses and only telling a filtered version of your story, the compliments and recognition you receive don't hold much value. You leave a lot of attack surface for The Impostor to tell you that those opinions don't count; they aren't valid because those people don't know the whole story.

But when you tell your real story—the fully authentic version, in which you win *and* lose, succeed *and* fail, and feel confidence *and* fear—the respect you earn also feels real and authentic. When people tell you that you've done well, or that they admire you, or that you have inspired them, you know that they're talking about the real you and not a phony.

When that happens, you leave no room for The Impostor to attack and erode the encouragement you received. Admiration truly feels like admiration because it's authentic. Appreciation truly feels like appreciation. Encouragement truly feels like encouragement.

So the key to combating The Impostor is not just community; it's community with vulnerability. The vulnerability is critical. In fact, community *without* vulnerability will feed The Impostor, but community *with* vulnerability will starve it.

The Thing You Fear Is Exactly the Thing You Need

Ironically, The Impostor will cause you to fear being vulnerable. The Impostor will tell you that you can't open up and be honest about your weaknesses and flaws, about the areas where you are insecure or uncertain, because that puts you at risk. Impostor syndrome is rooted in a fear of being exposed, but being exposed is exactly the antidote to impostor syndrome!

> Community *without* vulnerability will feed The Impostor, but community *with* vulnerability will starve it.

A few years ago, my wife and I moved out of a subdivision to a home with a two-and-a-half-acre yard. I decided to buy a zero-turn lawn mower and cut the grass myself rather than pay someone to take care of it. I'm not much of an outdoor work–type of guy, so this was new territory for me.

My inexperience with outdoor equipment is a bit of a running joke among our circle of friends. Several of them own construction businesses and are comfortable building things and using heavy machinery, and they know that's not my area of expertise. They were helpful, though, with advice on what to buy and what to avoid, so I felt good about my purchase.

Within the first few minutes of my first time on the mower, I got stuck. I drove it a little too close to the ditch along the road, and one of the wheels dropped in a hole, where it just spun with no traction. It's far too heavy to lift or push by hand, so the only way to get it unstuck is to pull it out with another vehicle, but I didn't own anything with a tow hitch at the time.

Though I have several friends with big trucks who could easily pull it out, I didn't want to call them! I just knew I'd never hear the end of this story—five minutes on a mower and already stuck in a ditch. But I needed to get the job done, so I swallowed my pride and made the call.

A week later, when a bunch of our friends were all together, someone mentioned the incident. I braced myself for the jokes to start flying, but I was surprised by the reactions.

"I get mine stuck all the time."

"Me too."

"I have to pull my mower out of the ditch about once a month."

"You just bought this property. It'll take some time to learn where all the tricky spots are."

Turns out, it wasn't nearly as big a blunder as I'd made it out to be in my head. Talking openly with my friends about my mistake didn't make me feel worse; it actually made me feel better.

The Impostor wants to use your community—your circles of relationships—against you. It wants you to keep your guard up and hide your weaknesses and failures out of fear. It wants you to make assumptions about what people think, or will think, of you if they know the truth. And it wants those assumptions to be bad.

But by opening up and being real—being vulnerable—with the people around you, you'll unlock the value in those relationships. You'll both get and give encouragement and will learn a lot in the process.

But doing that well, and doing it consistently, is going to require a change in the way you think. It's going to require a change in your view of failure and a change in your view of success. It's going to require you to become an *Explorer*.

Things to Consider

Before moving on, take a few minutes to think about and answer these questions.

- Risk-takers and high achievers see the world differently than the average person and can struggle to build quality relationships as a result. How connected are you to similar people who share your goals as well as your challenges?
- Finding a great community sometimes takes work. You have to put in the effort to find it and get connected. What communities are available to you that you're not taking advantage of?

- Vulnerability is the key to making community work for you rather than against you. How difficult is it for you to be vulnerable and honest with your peers?
- The fear of rejection or ridicule can hold us back from being vulnerable, but it's often a baseless fear. If you were honest with the people around you about your strengths *and* your weaknesses—your successes *and* failures—what is the worst thing that could happen? What's the best thing that could happen?

SEVEN

Be an Explorer, Not a Tour Guide

By 2013 I had been running my consulting company for several years, and we'd hit some significant milestones in my mind. We had weathered the recession, had seven figures in annual revenue, opened a permanent office, and I had personally gotten to the point that I was doing very little client-facing consulting work, spending the majority of my time running the business.

One of my team members was acting as an interim CIO for one of our clients. It was no surprise to me when they offered her the job on a permanent basis. That happened a lot. We used to joke internally that if you'd been with a client for more than two weeks and they hadn't tried to hire you away, you must be doing something wrong.

I was a little surprised, though, at how much money they offered her. It was more than I could match, and she decided to take the job.

And then, another key member of my team got an offer and took it. And another. And another.

In the space of less than a year, I had two thirds of my team hired away by a couple of clients with deep pockets. Though I was happy for each individual and the opportunity that was given them, it was a difficult time for my company and for me personally.

I had an overwhelming feeling of failure.

And of course, The Impostor jumped on it:

"See—this was never a real business in the first place."

"You're not a leader if people don't continue to follow you."

"You can find great people, but you can't keep them."

"You've just gotten lucky all these years, and now your luck has run out."

"You're in over your head. You can't do this."

"You now have a failure on your permanent record as an entrepreneur."

No actual person said any of these things to me, but I believed that people saw me this way. It seemed obvious. If I couldn't hold a team together, I must not be a very good leader, right?

I spent the next year or so struggling with what to do next. Do I rebuild the team? What if that happens again? What if it was all my fault? Am I difficult to work for? Will anyone even want to work for me if they hear about the exodus?

I remember during that time being introduced by someone as a "successful entrepreneur," but I didn't feel like a success at all. I felt like I had failed. I didn't want to tell my story. I didn't want anyone to ask about my business. I even struggled to accept the title *entrepreneur* because I didn't think I was in the same category as the other entrepreneurs I knew.

The Fear of Failure

"Success is failure in progress."

—Albert Einstein

Too many people see failure as something to avoid. They believe that failure is the opposite of success. It certainly feels that way in the moment! No one experiences failure and thinks, *This is awesome. Where can I get some more?*

But failure is not the *opposite* of success; failure is *part* of success. It's a step in the process. No one has ever achieved anything great without some failures along the way.

There's a famous story among IBM employees, of Tom Watson Jr. when he was running the company many years ago. Watson had called one of his vice presidents into his office to discuss a failed development project that cost IBM somewhere in the range of $10 million (many times that number in today's dollars).

Expecting to be fired, the VP came to the office with his letter of resignation in hand. Tom Watson Jr. looked at the letter, shook his head, and responded, "Why would we let you go? We just invested $10 million in your education."

Failure is only truly failure if you learn nothing. In fact, we learn more from failures than we do from success, and when we brush those failures under the rug or try to gloss over them, we rob ourselves, and those around us, of the valuable wisdom that comes with that experience.

Babe Ruth is considered one of the greatest baseball players of all time. He was called The Sultan of Swat and held numerous Major League Baseball records, including career home runs, runs batted in (RBIs), slugging percentage, and several others. Some of his records still stand at the time I'm writing this book.

> Failure is only truly failure if you learn nothing.

Do you know what his other nickname was? The King of Strikeouts. His career total of 1,330 strikeouts was the Major League Baseball record for thirty years until it was finally beaten by none other than Mickey

Mantle. Babe Ruth did great things because he took big chances—and not just in private. He did it on the big stage, with thousands of people watching.

> *"Never let the fear of striking out get in your way."*
>
> —Babe Ruth

Abraham Lincoln failed in business, had a nervous breakdown, and suffered multiple political defeats before being elected president of the United States.

Steve Jobs was fired from Apple, the company he founded, only to come back years later and save it from going under.

> *"I have not failed 10,000 times. I have not failed once. I have succeeded in proving that those 10,000 ways will not work. When I have eliminated the ways that will not work, I will find the way that will work."*
>
> —Thomas Edison, on his many attempts to create the first electric lightbulb

Before creating his namesake company, Walt Disney's Laugh-O-Gram Studio went bankrupt, and he was fired from a Missouri newspaper for not being creative enough.

Colonel Harland Sanders failed at nearly everything he had tried before creating the secret recipe for Kentucky Fried Chicken at age 65.

Dr. Seuss intended to earn his PhD in literature from Lincoln College, Oxford, but failed and eventually dropped out of school. His first book, *And to Think I Saw It on Mulberry Street*, was rejected twenty-eight times. By the time he died in 1991, he had sold over 600 million copies of his books in twenty different languages.

> *"I've missed more than 9,000 shots in my career. I've lost almost 300 games. Twenty-six times I've been trusted to take the game-winning shot and missed. I've failed over and over and over again in my life. And that is why I succeed."*
>
> —Michael Jordan

Henry Ford's first company went bankrupt, and his second company also went south when, after a dispute with partners, he was forced to walk away with only the rights to his name.

Before his move into milk chocolate, Milton Hershey had started several candy companies that ultimately failed. He reached the point that his own family refused to lend him any money because of his string of failures.

Every success story includes failures along the way. They're part of the process.

Don't Be a Tour Guide

Some people let the fear of failure (and especially the fear of public failure) put limits on their lives and careers. They believe that in order to feel confident, they must have already succeeded and must have all the answers. They need to have "been there, done that" before they can lead or teach others. I call them Tour Guides.

Tour Guides stick to a well-worn path, taking people only where they are familiar. They avoid unknown territory in order to maintain their confident image.

Tour Guides are afraid to admit they haven't been somewhere before. They believe their expertise will be called into question if they show the slightest bit of uncertainty. To maintain their feeling of control, they put tight boundaries around their world and make the same basic loop again and again.

Are you a Tour Guide? Here are some of the signs. Tour Guides

- are most confident when they're the most knowledgeable person in the group;
- answer most questions themselves, without seeking other opinions;
- only ask a question when they already know the answer;
- avoid unfamiliar or uncomfortable topics; and
- stick to the plan, even if it's no longer relevant—they don't adapt.

Tour Guides separate leading and learning into two distinct activities and are either doing one or the other, but rarely both at the same time.

When Tour Guides are confronted by The Impostor, they work hard to prove it wrong; they use their script, knowledge, and familiarity to combat insecurity. They avoid situations where The Impostor's voice is strong and stay in the safe zones where they have the upper hand.

Tour Guides let their fear of failure dominate and limit their choices. They believe that failure is fatal, that it's a permanent mark on their record. Failure has to be avoided because it is not easily overcome. So they do the same tour, over and over.

Be an Explorer—It's Much More Fun!

"It is better to make a thousand failures than to be too cowardly to ever undertake anything."
—Clovis G. Chappell

Other people choose to be more adventurous. I call them Explorers. They're willing to move in directions they've never moved in before, and they lean into situations where they might not be the expert or even have much knowledge.

Explorers aren't concerned with *having* all the answers; they're focused on *finding* the answers. They aren't afraid to say, "I don't know; let's figure that out together," or "Does anyone else have more experience here?" They're not only willing to admit when they are in new territory, they're excited about the opportunity to explore, grow, and learn.

What are the characteristics of an Explorer? Explorers

- ask more questions than they answer
- ask questions in order to learn rather than to instruct or correct,
- lean in to uncomfortable or unfamiliar territory, and
- start with a plan, but are open and willing to change for the better.

This approach is so much more fun! It's exciting, adventurous, and at times even terrifying. There's so much more to learn as an Explorer and so much more to accomplish.

It's not that Explorers never experience fear. They're not superheroes who are invincible. They manage their fear and harness that energy to push through challenges rather than back up from them.

Explorers don't avoid The Impostor; they disarm it. By being open to continual learning, they avoid the stress of not having the answers. By embracing failure as part of success, they take the threat of failure out of The Impostor's playbook.

The Impostor has no power over a confident Explorer. It may be present, but the Explorer can acknowledge it and move forward anyway.

Entrepreneurs and leaders need to be Explorers. We have to take risks and break new ground. We must try things, even when success is far from certain. That means we will make a lot of mistakes along the way. We sometimes spend a lot of energy going in a certain direction, only to learn that it was a dead end, and now we have to go back.

> The Impostor has no power over a confident Explorer.

But The Impostor is always trying to turn us into a Tour Guide by telling us that failure is fatal and that uncertainty makes us weak. It tries to convince us to play it safe, to avoid any situation where we might have to double back and admit we were wrong. It wants us to manage and protect our image at the expense of learning and growing.

Maintaining an Explorer's mentality is crucial. It gives you the freedom to take risks and the confidence to lean in to those risks.

Anyone who is going to attempt something great is going to experience failure. When you take a lot of swings, you're going to have a lot of misses, but that's the Explorer way. Explorers try things, learn what doesn't work, and get better in the process.

How to Shift from Tour Guide to Explorer

James was both a successful entrepreneur, having built an IT services company to the point that it could run without his day-to-day involvement, and a specialized technology consultant. He'd been able to move from client to client, working on the projects that interested and challenged him most.

He was eventually recruited by a large global technology consulting firm. Though he'd enjoyed working with much smaller companies, it was a good opportunity that he felt he should pursue.

It wasn't long, though, before the stresses of the new job were weighing on him. In particular, the company had tasked him with creating an entirely new line of business, something they'd never had before.

"I feel a lot of pressure to have the answers," he told me. "They're looking to me to tell them how this new line of business should work, but this is something I've never done before. I don't know what to say most of the time."

Even though James had been completely honest with his new employer about his experience, he was still struggling with impostor syndrome, the feeling that his bosses and coworkers saw more in him than was actually there and that he was at risk of being exposed.

As we talked about his strengths and the reasons he took this job in the first place, it was clear that James had spent much of his career as an Explorer. He had experimented, tried, failed, learned, built, and adapted his way to success.

But something was different here. Something about this company and this particular job had made him think like a Tour Guide, and he genuinely feared that he wasn't going to make it. He thought that he had hit some kind of limit, that he had moved into a position that was too big for him. He was feeling the pressure to give a well-rehearsed, expert tour of how this new line of business should work, and he was falling short of that expectation.

The light bulb moment came when he realized that he had put that expectation on himself.

The reason he had been recruited and hired by this huge firm was not that he had done *this* before, but because he had done *so many other things* before. He was a creator, a problem solver, and an innovator. They hadn't hired him to do the same thing over again; they had hired him to do something new, and that's what he was good at doing.

"They didn't hire me to have the answers. They hired me to find the answers." It was as though a huge weight had been lifted off his shoulders. He stopped thinking like a Tour Guide, where a lack of knowledge is a weakness, and started thinking like an Explorer. The things he didn't know were the opportunities to shine rather than flaws to be covered up.

It happened in a moment, in one conversation, but the change was dramatic. He got comfortable saying, "I don't know" or giving an opinion that was off the cuff and not completely scrutinized. A month later, James told me that his relationships at work had improved, his ideas were flowing, and his boss had even commented about the difference in his work and his attitude. He was exploring again!

Think Differently About Failure

My business had seven years of consistent growth, followed by a major setback (losing more than half my team). Does that one setback erase the years of success? It seemed like it at the time, but of course, in hindsight, the answer is no.

Just because you *had* a failure does not mean that you *are* a failure. Failure is just one step on the road to success. Adopting the Explorer mentality allows you to take those failures, extract all the experience that comes with them, and continue exploring!

The next step, after changing the way you think about failure, is to redefine success. We are bombarded with messages about what success looks like and what it means to everyone else. Don't make the mistake of building on others' definition of success. You have to define it for yourself.

Just because you
***had* a failure does not**
mean that you
***are* a failure.**

Things to Consider

Before moving on, take a few minutes to think about and answer these questions.

- Tour Guide thinking—playing it safe, avoiding failure, and focusing on maintaining an image instead of learning and growing—tempts us all at one time or another. In what area of your life have you been thinking and acting like a Tour Guide? How can you change that?
- Many people fear failure, but failure is a great teacher, and we usually learn more from failure than we do from success. When was the last time you failed and learned a valuable lesson in the process?
- The fear of failure holds us back until we recognize how valuable failure can be. What would you do differently if you believed that failure was a big step toward success?
- Learning and teaching are not mutually exclusive; you can actually do both at the same time. When was the last time you taught someone something that you were still learning yourself? Is there an opportunity for you to do that now?

EIGHT

Redefine Success

A few years into my entrepreneurial journey, I sat in a hotel lobby, waiting for the beginning of the conference I had flown in to attend. I couldn't help but overhear the conversation between two men sitting nearby. One of them was obviously a businessman and was several years—maybe even a couple of decades—older than I was.

"I'm making some changes," I heard him say. "I'm really trying to slow down and reconnect with my family. I've traveled all over the world, made millions of dollars, and done these huge business deals, but now I need to work on my marriage, and I barely have a relationship with my children, who are all grown up."

I remember thinking immediately, *What do I need to do to make sure that I never, ever say that?*

I had two realizations that morning. First, all success comes with a cost. Success requires sacrifice. In order to say *yes* to one thing, you have to say *no* to many other things, and it's really important to recognize that and be intentional about what you're willing to turn down. The second realization was that I usually have no idea what another person has chosen to sacrifice in pursuit of their success.

Don't Fall into the Comparison Trap

My friend Mark is a husband, a father, and a business owner. He had started his business at twenty-three years old and had created a business model that was more than a decade ahead of the rest of his industry. Most people who looked at him would have called him successful.

But Mark had a big problem: his brother-in-law, Kevin. Mark had married a woman whose brother was also an entrepreneur and was even in the same industry. Kevin had built and sold a company hundreds of times the size of Mark's business.

At first blush, that might seem like a great advantage, but rather than look at it as an opportunity to learn,

Mark felt the pressure of comparing himself to Kevin and worried constantly that he didn't measure up.

> In order to say *yes* to one thing, you have to say *no* to many other things.

"I always felt insecure. I always felt inferior," he told me. "My kids would always hate going over to Uncle Kevin's because I became a different person."

Mark could only see his accomplishments lined up against Kevin's accomplishments, and that left him feeling inadequate rather than confident.

"I felt totally unworthy."

What Mark didn't know until years later was that Kevin's accomplishments had come at a cost. Kevin had his own set of struggles—his own personal demons to battle—and he had his own set of insecurities as well. All that "success" was just what was visible from the outside. There was a lot more baggage underneath the surface.

> When we compare ourselves to others, we're judging the reality of our own lives against a filtered version of theirs.

This is one of the basic problems with being realistic about our own success: We use the wrong measuring stick, comparing ourselves to others who appear successful. Whenever we compare ourselves to others, we're judging the reality of our own lives against a highly filtered and polished version of theirs.

Unfortunately, technology, and particularly social media, has amplified this problem. Most successful people only post about their wins, not their losses. Social networks are full of carefully crafted and edited images of people's lives and careers.

Rarely, if ever, do we know someone else's complete story. We may see their accomplishments, but we don't know the personal sacrifices they may have made to get there. We experience their confidence, but have no idea what personal demons they may be wrestling.

You might compare yourself to someone who seems to have unlimited energy and rarely sleeps, only to find that they're abusing dangerous and addictive drugs to maintain that energy or that their lack of sleep now may take years off the end of their life.

You might compare yourself to someone who has a commanding presence and seems to get a lot done, but you may not realize that they leave a wake of broken relationships and disgruntled former team members behind them everywhere they go.

You might compare yourself to those accomplished businesspeople who have traveled the world and earned millions of dollars, only to find that their family relationships are frayed.

My point is not to tear down or criticize other people's success and it's not to try to convince you which sacrifices are appropriate and which are not. My point is that you simply don't know the full story behind another person's *apparent* success, so measuring yourself against it is never going to be accurate.

Discover the Real Measures of Success

Measuring success is not inherently bad. It's when we choose the wrong measures and fall into the comparison trap that it becomes destructive.

How, then, should we measure success? I've boiled down my criteria to three Ps: progress, passion, and purpose.

Measure Your Own Progress

Since measuring yourself against another person is never going to be accurate, the only reliable way to measure your success is against yourself. Are you making progress?

"Progress toward what?" you might ask. Well, that's where it becomes personal.

You and I likely do not have the same goals. We may not share the same values. So it would be foolish of me to tell you what you should be making progress toward, but it's clear to me that you should be making progress toward something.

Consider these questions.

- What have you learned recently?
- What habits have you changed or are you working to change?
- What skill are you developing or refining?
- What is something that you used to find difficult but now can do easily?
- What is something that you still find difficult but would like to do easily?
- Is there a subject of which you have little knowledge but would like to know more?
- Is there a subject in which you would like to move from knowledge to expertise?
- What underdeveloped talents do you have?
- With what part of your life are you the least satisfied, and what is one thing you can do to improve that?

Notice that none of these great questions have anything to do with comparing yourself to another person.

The ability to set goals for yourself—goals that are challenging but achievable—and then to work toward those goals is a definition of success that is independent of what anyone else is doing.

There's no reason for you to feel like an impostor if you're living your own life and succeeding at that!

Follow Your Own Passions

A second metric of success, which is admittedly more subjective, is this: How much of your life and your work is in line with your passions?

Are you regularly doing work that excites you, or are you trying to get through it most of the time?

None of us gets to *only* do things that we love. Life is full of chores and tasks and obstacles that get in the way of enjoying every minute. But if you can move more of your life and work to be in line with your passions, you will be living a more successful life.

Consider these questions.

- Of all the work that you do, what brings you the most joy?
- What motivates you to get out of bed in the morning?

- What would you attempt if you knew you could not fail?
- If you were going to make the same amount of money, no matter what job you chose, what type of work would you choose to do?
- If your work was completely done in secret and only you knew about it (there was no public recognition), what would you choose to do?
- If you could instantly become an expert at one thing, what would that be?

When you're doing work that you love—when you're excited and intrinsically motivated to do what you're doing—there's no need to compare yourself to other people. In fact, that would be foolish because they don't have the same passions that you do!

Even more importantly, when you're doing work that you love, you can find joy and pleasure in the work itself. The work is not a means to an end; it's not just a way to earn money so that you can enjoy your life. The work itself is the joy. You can take pleasure in your work, and the money you earn and the life you build with that money are just the cherries on top.

Discover and Fulfill Your Purpose

The third and most important measure of success is to what degree you are fulfilling your purpose.

Success literally means "the accomplishment of an aim or purpose." You were put on this earth for a reason, and no other person was made to fill your role. Are you walking in your purpose, or are you trying to fill another person's role?

You are the only you who exists in this world. But when you try to live another person's life—when you try to fulfill their purpose instead of your own—you not only struggle (and ultimately fail) in that pursuit, but you deprive the world of *your* unique purpose.

I have been a Christian all my life, and I believe that God created each one of us with a purpose and a plan. When I am living outside of that plan and purpose, I grow frustrated and dissatisfied, always looking for something else to fill the gap in my life. But when I am fulfilling my purpose, I feel peace, joy, and great satisfaction.

How do you know if you're living in your purpose? Here's the first clue: Your purpose is *never* about *you*.

If your driving motivation for the work you do is to make a lot of money and create a comfortable life for yourself, you are probably not fulfilling your purpose. I'm not saying that it's wrong to build wealth or to enjoy the rewards of your work; it's perfectly OK to do both. But that's not why you're here.

> Your purpose
> is *never*
> about *you.*

Your purpose is always about something more and bigger than you. It's not necessarily easy or obvious. Some people spend years, and even decades, searching for their purpose. But there is a reason you are on this earth, and you need to find that reason and pursue it.

Zack was a salesperson for a large home improvement company, and though he made good money, he was miserable most of the time. He remembered volunteering at a mission downtown when he was younger and had dreamed of starting a business that could employ people who were fighting to get out of tough situations—people who were homeless, recovering from addiction, and reformed convicts.

He finally saved up enough money to quit his sales job and launch the company. Though it was tough getting it off the ground, and he didn't make as much money as he had in sales, he was so much happier because he knew that his life meant something, and he was making a difference.

Until you do the inner work of discovering and understanding your purpose, it will be difficult to find satisfaction in the outer work that you do.

Manage Your Perfectionism (but Don't Eliminate It)

Growing up, I struggled with perfectionism. I could never get myself motivated to do something unless I was confident I could do it really well. (I had a Tour Guide mentality.) I remember in third or fourth grade, my school had a science fair, and I was supposed to enter a project as part of my grade for the year.

Though there were plenty of things I could have done, I couldn't think of an idea that I was sure would win the top prize. I didn't want to do one of the standard experiments that had been done over and over by kids for years. I wanted to be unique and special.

So I just didn't do it. I skipped the science fair entirely and got a zero on the assignment. Looking back, I realize what a mistake that was. The purpose wasn't winning; it was learning, and because I didn't think I could win, I refused to learn.

Fast forward thirty-five years, and one of my sons was dealing with the same dilemma. He's a brilliant kid but isn't satisfied with just doing something run of the mill. He was required to submit a project to his school's science fair but didn't want to do it because he couldn't think of a great idea.

Every suggestion we gave him he dismissed as unoriginal or uninteresting, but we kept pushing. My wife and I weren't going to let him make the same mistake that I did.

He finally came up with an idea and spent a week on the experiment, only to have it completely fail. He didn't get the wrong results; he got no results. Something had gone wrong, and he had nothing to submit.

With only twenty-four hours to go until his experiment was due, we pushed him to get creative. We brainstormed a handful of ideas that could be done in one day and forced him to pick one.

He barely got it done in time, but we went to the science fair and set up his exhibit. He was pleasantly surprised when people took an interest in his work, and even more so when he won second place in his age group.

The valuable lesson that he learned didn't come from the experiment he chose, the results he generated, or the poster he displayed. It came from pushing through failure without giving up, and it came through making a choice and moving forward, even though the choice wasn't an obvious winner. It came when he gave up on perfection in favor of progress.

Best of all, he was proud of his second-place win, and so was I. It's certainly much better than the zero that I got when I was a kid.

Psychologists categorize perfectionists into two different types.[7] Normal perfectionists have high standards and may be disappointed when they don't measure up to those standards, but they are still able to take pleasure in their results. Normal, or "healthy," perfectionism doesn't erode self-esteem.

Neurotic perfectionists, on the other hand, set very high, often unrealistic, standards for themselves and then feel dissatisfied and disappointed when they can't achieve those standards. That's the way I approached the science fair as a kid. The only result I would be happy with was the top prize, and if I didn't think I could get there, it wasn't worth doing at all.

Studies have shown that impostor syndrome is correlated with neurotic perfectionism. That is, people who have unhealthy perfectionistic standards *and* cannot be satisfied with any result that falls short of those standards are likely to suffer from impostor syndrome.

It's OK to set high standards for yourself and create some lofty goals. It's even OK to let your failure to meet those standards serve as motivation to drive you to improve. But it's also important to allow yourself to enjoy and appreciate what you accomplish along the way.

A few years into my consulting business, we had about $350,000 in revenue for the year, and I set a goal of $1 million for the following calendar year. This was a boutique consulting firm, not a high-growth tech company, so that was a lofty goal.

When I shared the goal with one of my executive coaches, he said, "I'd rather you aim for the stars and hit the moon than play it safe and reach your goals every time."

That year, we did $580,000 in revenue. We did more than $1 million the following year.

Though we didn't hit the million-dollar goal the first time, I was happy to have 65 percent growth that year, and it set us up well for another 70-plus percent growth the following year. I could have allowed myself to be upset or disappointed that we didn't make it the first time, but that wouldn't have made any difference. What was done was done, and all we could do was learn from it and move forward. It was still a successful year by most measures.

The key to keeping perfectionism in check is to allow yourself to be satisfied, and even gratified, when you hit the moon rather than the stars.

Receive (and Enjoy) the Praise

My friend Matt is a writer, with three number-one best sellers and millions of books sold over the course of his career. But he has a hard time receiving compliments on his work. Whenever anyone pays him a

The key to keeping perfectionism in check is to allow yourself to be satisfied, and even gratified, when you hit the moon rather than the stars.

compliment or tells him they read one of his books, he has a standard response that goes something like, "Oh, so it was you and Mom who read that one."

One of the symptoms of impostor syndrome is not being able to accept a compliment at face value. Instead, you deflect the compliment with sarcasm or downplay the importance of whatever you did.

"It's not that big a deal."

"I didn't really have that much to do with it."

"The bar is low."

"You must be my other fan, alongside my mother."

Have you ever considered that when someone pays you a compliment and you deflect or diffuse it, you are actually insulting them? What you're really saying is that their opinion isn't valid, or their standards are too low, or they just don't know what they're talking about.

Often, it's an attempt to appear (or to genuinely be) humble. By downplaying the compliment, you're showing that you're not full of pride. But that may not be the way it comes across to others. It might actually seem arrogant or at least insulting.

Acting humble is not always a sign of humility. In fact, false humility is a form of pride. Note that I'm not talking about healthy pride, like when you're proud of your children or proud of a job well done. I'm talking about the kind of pride that hurts you—the pride that prevents you from admitting when you're wrong or from asking for help when you need it.

> Acting humble is not always a sign of humility.

My wife, Mary, comes from a family with Amish roots. Though she wasn't raised Amish herself (both of her parents left the Amish way of life in their teenage years), some of her extended family are Amish, living without electricity and most other modern conveniences.

Though there are some great people in the Amish community, they're subject to human nature just like the rest of us. The running joke is that certain people among the Amish are very proud of their humility. They appear to be living a humble lifestyle, but there's actually a good deal of competitiveness as to who can be the most humble, as well as a judgmental attitude toward others who are less humble.

It's just pride in disguise. It's arrogance, cloaked in a false humility.

If you're working hard to *appear* humble, you're really just managing your image. That's not true humility; that's just another form of pride.

Move from Proud Insecurity to Humble Confidence

For years I struggled with pride and insecurity at the same time. I often felt like I was moving from one to the other so fast I was suffering from emotional whiplash.

One moment, I'd be confident, even arrogant, about my abilities as an entrepreneur, and then a short time later, I'd feel completely unsure of myself. I'd be overconfident with one group of people and intimidated by another group.

I eventually learned that outward pride is often a sign of inward insecurity. It's your brain's way of trying to overcompensate for fear. You act as if by simply bragging about yourself, you can erase your flaws and make yourself awesome. I call it "Proud Insecurity."

If you haven't felt this yourself, you've almost certainly been around someone who was outwardly prideful but clearly had some insecurities. In fact, it's usually a lot more obvious to others than we think it is.

When you're operating in Proud Insecurity, you're playing a role, acting out a character that's not really you. The *real* you is insecure, so you create this outward character who appears self-assured. You're like a professional wrestler who is mean and nasty when he's on screen but is actually a really nice guy in the dressing room before and after the show.

That persona—that false character that you're playing—is a barrier that will keep you from connecting with people in a real way. It'll prevent you from being vulnerable and will only feed The Impostor.

The emotional roller coaster of bouncing back and forth between pride and insecurity, going in and out of character, can wear you out. It's exhausting. And the resulting confusion leads to things like deflecting compliments with sarcasm or bragging about things that don't really mean much.

If Proud Insecurity is at one end of the spectrum, the opposite end is Humble Confidence, an outward humility combined with inner confidence.

It may seem like humility and confidence are opposites, but they're not. They actually work well together.

> *"Humility is not thinking less of yourself, but thinking of yourself less."*
>
> —C.S. Lewis

When you're inwardly confident, you don't have to be outwardly prideful. You don't have to create a character to play in order to mask what's going on inside. You can just be you, and be real and authentic. You spend a lot less energy managing your image and worrying about what others are thinking. That energy can go to much more productive work.

Proud Insecurity is like a high-wire act. It's a delicate balance, and the footing is bad. It takes constant effort because it's not natural. You have to move slowly and carefully to maintain that balance, and the cost of failure is high. When you fall, it's damaging and painful.

Humble Confidence, though, is a solid road—a stable, well-built foundation, where your footing is secure and you can move quickly and adapt easily. The

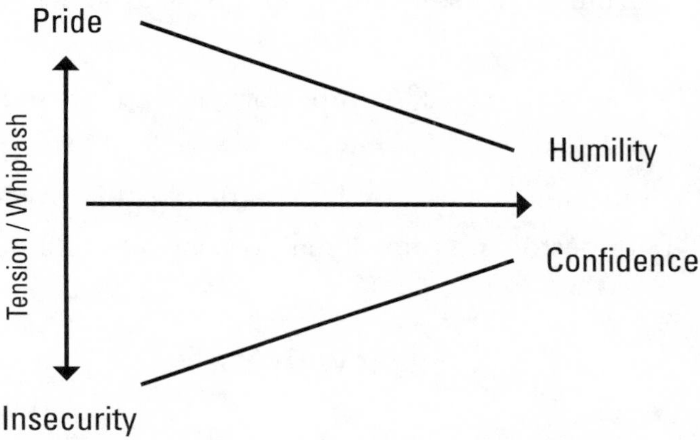

cost of failure, of tripping and falling, is low. You may get a few scrapes and bruises, but you'll be able to get right up and keep moving.

When you're Humbly Confident, you aren't spending any energy managing your image or worrying about what others are thinking. You can focus on much more important work.

Tour Guides often live in Proud Insecurity, presenting themselves as experts while secretly hoping no one will ask them a question that wasn't covered by their training.

Explorers, on the other hand, can be Humbly Confident. They are happy to give their opinion if asked, but they don't *need* to give it. They're more interested in learning new things than they are with showing off everything they know.

And of course, The Impostor has a playground in Proud Insecurity. The tension between how you act on the outside and how you feel on the inside just feeds The Impostor and provides all sorts of ammunition.

Say It with Me

There's a powerful phrase that can help you move from Proud Insecurity to Humble Confidence. This phrase is not only underused, it's actually avoided, and that avoidance is the source of many headaches and problems.

The phrase is simply, "I don't know."

Three little words. They seem so simple and clear and yet can be so difficult to force out of your mouth! Saying it feels like admitting a weakness, but it actually shows a great deal of strength. It takes strength and confidence to confess to not knowing something instead of hemming and hawing and beating around the bush, trying to come up with something that sounds intelligent.

When you say, "I don't know," you free yourself from the obligation to maintain an appearance, a false image of expertise. You all at once show humility (acknowledging a limitation) and confidence (not being afraid to admit your limitation).

You will usually gain people's respect more by saying "I don't know" than you will by avoiding saying it (especially when it's already obvious to those people that you don't know!). It's just another way of being vulnerable, and most people respect and appreciate it.

That doesn't mean we should say, "I don't know" all the time. Of course there are many times that we *do* know something. But we definitely should say it more than we want to. It's not a natural impulse; it's a habit that must be built and practiced.

Saying "I don't know" doesn't have to be the end of a sentence. You can say, "I don't know, but . . ." You can then share your ideas, or you can invite input from others, or you can talk about how you might go about researching, learning, and exploring.

Here's my challenge to you: The next time you are asked a question, before you answer it, pause and ask yourself, "Do I really know the answer to this, or am I about to take a guess?" If you know the answer, by all means, give it! But if you don't, start by saying that you don't know.

You can then talk about theories and ideas without the stress and pressure to come up with the right answer or even the one that just sounds right. You can spend less energy trying to look and sound like an expert and more energy exploring possibilities.

Success Means Becoming the Best Version of Yourself

The word *success* has a lot of hidden meaning behind it. Some people make it about money, while others equate it with fame, notoriety, influence, or control. For most people, it just means having what they see other people getting.

Don't fall into the comparison trap. Instead of trying to measure up to other people, focus on your own measures of success—your progress, passion, and purpose. If you are growing in the areas where you need to grow, not just trying to replicate another person's success, you'll become something that no one else can become: the best version of yourself.

The best version of yourself is one that is both humble and confident, and one that can receive and appreciate the compliments that others pay you. It's a version of you that sets high standards and works hard to meet those standards but doesn't beat yourself up when you only get to 80 percent of your goal. Instead, you learn from that experience and move forward, continuing to explore.

The best version of yourself is also not a lone ranger. You need to learn how to build your community—specifically, three types of community, which we will discuss in the next chapter—to surround yourself with the right people who will push you to grow while maintaining your humility and confidence.

Things to Consider

Before moving on, take a few minutes to think about and answer these questions.

- Measuring success against others is a trap because you can never really know the truth about that comparison. How have you defined and measured success in your career? Is it measured against others or against things you can truly understand, such as progress, passion, and purpose? How can you redefine your measures to make them more accurate?
- Do you know what your purpose is? Some people take years, even decades, to discover and truly understand their purpose. What

steps can you take to identify, learn about, and understand your purpose?

- Perfectionism can be healthy or unhealthy (neurotic), depending on whether you allow yourself to enjoy your success, even when you don't quite hit the mark. Do you set high standards for yourself? What happens when you fall short?

- Proud Insecurity is a dangerous, stressful pattern of thinking that can wear you out and undermine your success. Have you ever fallen into that trap? How can you begin to move toward Humble Confidence?

NINE

Explore Together

My brother loves to go scuba diving. I once asked him if he ever just went out on a whim and went for a short dive by himself, and he said, "No. One of the first rules of scuba diving is that you never dive alone."

It makes sense. There are just too many things that can go wrong, so having someone with you can mean the difference between life and death. Most risky activities are that way—you need people around you to protect against some of the risks.

Another friend of mine loves to go hiking. He was traveling alone for business and decided to go for a hike to explore the area during his downtime. As he started off on a trail, there was a sign that said, "Never hike alone."

He didn't think it was that big of a deal; he was an experienced hiker and didn't plan on doing anything especially dangerous. But a few more yards down the path, there was another sign that said, "Beware of rattlesnakes."

That changed his mind. He turned around and headed back.

Having people around you you can trust will help keep you safe. They can also make you better. Other people will see things you don't see and have experiences that you don't have.

> *"If you want to go fast, go alone. If you want to go far, go together."*
>
> *—African proverb*

Professional athletes always work as part of a team. Even in an individual sport, like tennis or golf, anyone worth watching will have a team of coaches, trainers, therapists, advisors, and other experts who help them navigate the risks and elevate their skills.

There's an old saying, "You can't read the label when you're inside the jar." Other people will have a perspective on your situation that you don't (and can't) have. They'll be able to tell you when you're pushing yourself too hard or not hard enough. They'll encourage you to take the risks you might be afraid to take and warn you when you *should* be afraid but aren't.

I've already mentioned a few of the people who've had an influence on my life and career. Mike Wharton pushed me to learn web design. John Levy gave me my first consulting gig. Tom Hill taught me the power of relationships and connected me with incredible people. Roger Hall helped me to manage my thinking. David Jones regularly pushed me outside of my comfort zone. There are many more.

I can't think of a single accomplishment of which I'm proud that didn't involve other people.

In chapter 6 I wrote about the importance of community and the even more critical ingredient of vulnerability to unlock the power of that community. Community comes in many forms, from one-on-one relationships to large gatherings of people who are sharing an experience, but there are a few specific types of community that I believe are the most important.

You Need These Three Types of Community

There are three types of people that you always need to have in your life. The combination of these three, with their different perspectives and sets of experience, will provide many of the tools you need to combat The Impostor. Each of these, in their own way, will expose the lies that The Impostor tells you and help you to recognize the times that you're not being Humbly Confident.

You can get away with only one or two, but in order to be well-rounded and to protect yourself on all sides, you should work to build all three.

1. Mentors Who Have Gone Before You

> *"Everybody needs a coach."*
>
> —Bill Gates

I'm using the term *mentor* to describe several different types of experts, including coaches, consultants, advisors, and teachers, as well as other leaders who will give you some of their time. These are people who help you by bringing expertise you don't have and by challenging you to become more than you currently are.

The following people can serve as mentors.

- *Advisors* bring outside experience and expertise, but they typically only provide (as the name suggests) advice.
- *Consultants* also bring specific expertise, but they usually do some work and produce some output for you.
- *Coaches* challenge you, train you, and hold you accountable.
- *Teachers* convey information in a way that is easy to understand and digest.

The important thing is that you learn to reach out for help when you need it and to recognize the opportunities you have to tap into those experts.

Sometimes, mentors come through relationships. When I started my first company, a consulting business, I reached out to Larry Powell, a consultant I had worked with years earlier and who had started his own consulting business along with two partners.

Larry agreed to have lunch with me and let me pepper him with questions. He helped me shape my thinking around how a consulting business works and what I should and shouldn't do. We met several times during my first year in business, and he was immensely helpful, giving me both advice and encouragement. He also made introductions to other experts who could help me with specific things like accounting and insurance.

When I transitioned a few years ago from running a business to coaching other leaders, I turned to a good friend, Michael Powers, who had made that same transition about three years before I did. Being able to learn from such a great and recent example has been a huge help.

Some mentors come in the form of a boss or someone else in formal authority. Mike Wharton, the business owner who tasked me with building my first website, saw something in me that I didn't even see in myself. He pushed me to learn and develop a new skill, knowing full well that it could open up doors for me to leave his company.

A mentor who works with you every day is incredibly valuable because he or she can see you in action rather than just listen to you talk about yourself.

Sometimes, you hire a mentor.

Michael Hyatt, the former CEO of Thomas Nelson Publishing and author of several books himself, has said that the secret to success in any area of life is to hire the best coaches and instructors you can afford.[8] He explains that sometimes, the best you can afford is a good book. Other times, you can afford to take a class or participate in some other kind of group learning. However, if you can afford to hire a coach to work with you one on one, that's what you should do.

When I started my first business, with about $3,500, I bought a stack of books and met with anyone who would give me advice in exchange for a cup of coffee or a meal. That's what my budget would allow. As my business grew, I joined membership organizations and peer groups. Eventually, I could afford to hire a coach.

I've had multiple executive coaches over the years, and they've challenged, inspired, and pushed me to do things I wouldn't have done on my own. There's immense value in having an outside voice to speak into your life with no stake in the game—someone who's not a shareholder or employee of your business but who is only focused on making you better.

When I set out to write this book, I hired a writing coach (and trust me, the book is better for it). When I wanted to improve my public speaking skills, I hired a team of coaches and experts to help me craft and rehearse my message. When I decided to become an executive coach, I hired a coach who specializes in coaching coaches!

I've come to believe that anything worth doing is worth investing in to get the right kind of help to do it well.

How to Hire a Coach

If you have the budget to hire a dedicated coach, there are several important factors to consider.

Are They Capable of Being Objective?

Though a mentor brings knowledge and experience that is valuable to you, they will also bring their own opinions and biases. A good mentor knows how to be objective—to step out of the situation personally and to set aside their preferences and tastes in favor of sound advice.

Objectivity also means that they won't always accept your version of a story as the truth. They'll challenge you to consider alternative viewpoints and to see things differently. They'll push you to set aside your own biases.

Do They Want the Best for You (Not Them)?

> *"The delicate balance of mentoring someone is not creating them in your own image, but giving them the opportunity to create themselves."*
>
> —Steven Spielberg

A good mentor or advisor has your best interest in mind at all times and is not in it for their own agenda. Though they may be paid for their time and expertise, they will not push you in any direction that is for their benefit more than it is for yours.

Be wary of mentors who try to relive their lives and careers vicariously through you. If their motive is to validate their own choices by repeating their success in your life or to correct the mistakes they've made by pushing you in the opposite direction, they do not have your best interest in mind. Their desire should be to help you make the best decisions for yourself, regardless of how those decisions compare to their own journey.

This might even mean telling you that the best thing for you is to find a different mentor. If there's another person who is a better fit or if there's some conflict of interest that makes it difficult for the mentor to be objective, they should be honest and tell you that, even if it means ending your mentoring relationship.

Do Your Personalities Fit?

One of the most important factors when choosing a coach or a mentor is that your personalities work well together.

That's not to say that your personalities should be the same; they should be complementary in many respects. But if they're too far apart, it may be difficult to communicate well and to make progress together.

- If you're an extreme introvert, working with an extroverted mentor may be frustrating. Though the mentor may challenge you to do things you wouldn't do on your own, they may not understand your reluctance to rush into social situations or your anxiety about large crowds of strangers.
- If you're a methodical, thoughtful, and measured decision maker, you may not work well with a mentor who is quick and decisive. They may not give you the time and space you need

to process information and make decisions at your own pace.

- On the other hand, if you are decisive, you might be frustrated by a mentor who is slow and methodical. You may benefit from someone who moves at a slightly slower pace, who can help you slow down and avoid some of the mistakes that can be made by moving too quickly. But a mentor who is too detailed may feel like a drag on your progress.
- If you are a verbal processor (someone who thinks out loud and explores ideas by talking them out), you need a mentor who will have the patience to listen and give you the space to work through your thoughts. Perhaps, though, you will also benefit from a mentor who will push you just enough to conclude your thoughts and move to a decision when your natural inclination might be to keep exploring.

In each of these examples, you can benefit from someone who is somewhat different than you are, but not extremely different. You want someone who will push you outside of your comfort zone without completely shoving you off a cliff.

I recommend that you talk to more than one person before hiring a coach or advisor and that you focus not just on their credentials, but on the personality fit. A person who is a great coach for someone else may not be the best coach for you.

Are They Skilled or Just Experienced?

> *"The best teacher is not the one who knows most but the one who is most capable of reducing knowledge to that simple compound of the obvious and wonderful."*
>
> —H.L. Mencken

Teaching, coaching, and mentoring are skills, and those skills are separate from the expertise in whatever is being taught. Just because someone is knowledgeable and experienced, that doesn't mean that they're great at communicating that knowledge and experience to others.

When a friend of mine was old enough to learn how to drive, her father took her out for a lesson. He had her watch while he turned the car on, put it in gear, and drove for a couple of miles.

Then they stopped, and he put her in the driver's seat. "Your turn," he told her.

As she struggled to get the manual transmission car into gear, he just sat and watched. After a minute or so, he asked, "What are you doing?"

"Trying to get the car into gear," she replied.

"Well, you're doing it wrong," he said.

After a few more minutes, he said, "Forget it. Switch seats." And he put the car into gear and drove them home. End of lesson.

He knew very well how to drive a car. He'd been doing it for decades. But that didn't mean he was great at passing that knowledge on to someone else.

I once heard an entrepreneur say, "There's no reason to hire a business coach. Just find someone who has done what you want to do, and ask them to be your mentor." That sounds simple enough, but you have to find someone who is not only experienced, but also has the right skill set to transfer that experience to you. Otherwise, you'll be as frustrated as my friend after her driving lesson.

2. Peer Groups to Walk Alongside You

> *"It's good to learn from your mistakes. It's better to learn from other people's mistakes."*
>
> —Warren Buffett

You need a group, a circle of peers who are on a similar journey as you are. These are the people who can identify with your struggles and help you reset your perspective. An ideal peer group for an entrepreneur is made up of a handful people from similarly sized but noncompetitive businesses.

The similar size is important, because the CEO of a $150 million company deals with a different set of challenges than a CEO of a $2 million company or an independent artist who is managing his or her own career. That's not to say that you can't learn and benefit from a person in a different size company than yours, but it can easily start to feel like a mentor–mentee relationship rather than a peer relationship.

For more than ten years, I've been part of The Alternative Board, first as a member, while I ran two different businesses, and eventually as a facilitator and coach. The group I currently lead is made up of business owners in Middle Tennessee, with companies ranging between $1 million and $10 million in revenue.

I remember the day that two of my members—one in IT services and another in HVAC and construction—came to the realization that they have similar business models and were both attempting to transform their models in the same way. Though neither of them is an expert in the other member's industry, there's a lot of shared learning and comparison of best practices that goes on between them.

I've seen a lot of different peer group models over the years, and I believe a good peer group shares three characteristics. Consider the following questions.

Is the Group Diverse?

It may seem at first that the best type of group would be made up of businesses (and owners) that are like yours (and you) in as many ways as possible. Although there's value in being able to compare your businesses directly to each other, I believe there's just as much value in learning from businesses that are different from each other.

The peer groups that I've been a member and facilitator of have included businesses across a wide range industries:

- Financial services
- Real estate
- IT services
- Live events
- Health care
- Construction
- Boat sales and service
- Software
- Automotive repair equipment
- Marketing
- Wealth management
- Nonprofits
- Television networks
- Funeral services
- Hazardous chemicals management
- Restaurants

I have learned something from every one of them, and the businesses I have run have benefitted from that broad view of what works and what doesn't across a wide variety of business models and product or service categories.

Just as important, I have been able to see the challenges that are common across most industries and the struggles that nearly all entrepreneurs face. It's given me a balanced and well-rounded perspective on business leadership.

Does the Group Share a Desire for Growth?

I once interviewed an entrepreneur who was interested in joining one of my peer groups. As I asked him about his goals, he said, "I don't want this company to get too big. I'm making about $100,000 per year now, and if I can get to $150,000, then that's probably enough for me."

Hard stop. He was not a fit for our group. It's not that his choices are wrong; he can do with his company what he wants. It's that our group was made up of entrepreneurs who were focused on growing businesses, not putting limits on that growth.

You can't take a journey with people who want to sit still. You need to travel with people who want to move at a similar pace and who want to go the distance. That doesn't mean you have to all be building the same type of business or have the exact same long-term goals. It just means that people who are content to plateau and coast are not going to push you to grow, and vice versa.

Had he joined our group, the advice and challenges he would have received would have been counter to his goals, and he would not have provided the push that other members expected from their peers.

Is the Group Transparent Enough?

One business owner who joined one of my peer groups was surprised at the level of detail we would share with one another about our businesses, including financials, personnel issues, and risks we had to deal with.

"I was part of one of these groups before," he told me, "but I quit, because it was usually just a bunch of guys bragging to each other about how much money they're making, or comparing their 'stuff'—the houses, boats, vacations, etc. There wasn't any real, honest problem solving going on, because everyone was too obsessed with maintaining an image."

You absolutely must have transparency (and vulnerability) among your group, or it will mostly be a waste of your time. If you're there to try to prove that you are as good or better than everyone else, you're going to go into Tour Guide mode, talking about everything you're doing right and avoiding the areas where you need improvement. If everyone in the group is in

Tour Guide mode, there won't be much learning or improving going on at all.

On the other hand, if everyone is willing to open up and be real about where they stand and what they need to improve, you have a real chance of growing together. You can operate as a group of Explorers, each benefiting from the things you are all learning.

This is also the reason that you need to be in a peer group without competitors and preferably without any vendor–customer relationships. You need to feel comfortable being yourself and talking about your struggles.

3. Mentees Will Learn from You (but You Learn Too)

> *"We make a living by what we get; we make a life by what we give."*
>
> —Winston Churchill

No matter where you are on your journey, someone else can learn from your experience. If you've only taken the first two steps, there's someone else who has only taken one and is trying to figure out step two.

Too many people believe that mentoring and teaching are things you can only do in the late years of your life and career, that you have to accomplish most of the things you want to accomplish before you can help other people along their journey. That's Tour Guide thinking.

I believe that you can, and should, always be mentoring. Imagine yourself climbing a hill, with both arms outstretched—one uphill, to get help from someone on higher ground, and one downhill, to help the person behind you. That's my view of mentoring. I am always in need of help and always able to help. It's

not an either/or proposition, and each one makes the other more meaningful.

In the same way that mentors come in different forms and through different types of relationships, so do mentees. You might have an employee who can use some personal guidance and encouragement. You might have a friend or colleague who is starting their journey a few years behind you and can benefit from your experience. You might work with a nonprofit or an educational institution to teach and train others.

For years I've been an advisor and teacher at the Nashville Entrepreneur Center. It's a voluntary position where I teach classes and provide help and advice to early-stage entrepreneurs. Some of the entrepreneurs I advised in the early years are now advisors themselves, working alongside me to help other entrepreneurs.

I recognized early in my entrepreneurial journey that several people had helped me along the way, to whom I had little to offer. They were further down the road than I was and much more experienced than I was. Though I might one day be able to do them some sort of favor, the chances were just as likely that they'd be retired or that we'd lose touch before I would have that opportunity.

Instead of trying to figure out ways that I could pay them back, I decided to focus on paying it forward. I made a decision that I would always build into my schedule and my priorities the time to spend with people who can't offer much to me.

What I learned, though, is that mentoring is rarely one-sided. I have sometimes gotten as much or more out of my time helping another person as they did. It's been said that if you want to master something, teach it. I've definitely learned as much by teaching and mentoring as I have by being a student or mentee.

Manage These Relationships Like Valuable Assets

The biggest mistake I made during my first two years as an entrepreneur was not spending enough time building relationships. I was fortunate to be quite busy with client work, but I focused almost entirely on generating revenue and didn't spend much time with anyone who was not a paying (or potential) client.

When the Great Recession hit hard in 2009, my client workload completely dried up, and I was suddenly alone. The need to find new clients drove me to do a lot of networking during the following year. In fact, for nearly ten months, that was just about the only thing I did.

During that time, though, I began to realize that I needed people in my life who could do more than just help me find customers. I needed people who could help me to become better—better at serving my clients, a better business owner, and a better leader.

The combination of these three sets of relationships—mentors, peers, and mentees—will simultaneously challenge and push you to grow, while keeping you grounded and realistic. They'll help you see that you have both a lot to offer *and* a lot to learn. They'll help you to be both humble and confident.

But these relationships don't always happen naturally; you have to be intentional about them. Individual people will move in and out of these circles over time, but you should always work to maintain these three types of community and keep these valuable relationships strong.

Things to Consider

Before moving on, take a few minutes to think about and answer these questions.

- Most successful people can name one or more people who have contributed to their success. Who are the most important mentors who have helped you on your journey? When was the last time you thanked them? What can you do to show your appreciation?
- Your chances of success are increased by sharing your journey with others who are working toward some of the same goals and learning some of the same lessons that you are. What types of people would you want to be in your peer group? Do you already know some of them? Where can you meet even more?
- You have something valuable to offer to others, even if you haven't achieved everything you are working toward. Who are some people in your life who could benefit from your experience? What can you do to offer them help and encouragement? How can you make that a habit?

TEN

Facing The Impostor with Every New Season

During the time that I was researching and writing this book, I spoke to hundreds of entrepreneurs. A vast majority of the time, when I explained what I was working on, I'd get great feedback on the idea and need for a guide that addresses impostor syndrome for entrepreneurs and leaders.

And then there was Greg. An entrepreneur himself, Greg was running a public relations company, specifically, one that helped experts get booked as guests on television programs, podcasts, and so on. We were introduced to each other by another one of his clients and were just getting acquainted and learning about what each of us was working on.

Greg had never heard of impostor syndrome and asked me to explain it to him. When I did, he said, "Wow, I can't think of a single entrepreneur who feels that way. Entrepreneurs are confident. *I don't think that anyone will buy that book.*"

Ouch! That hurt. He just told me I'd wasted months and months of work. I wanted to tell him he was an idiot and to back that up with all the research, and all the interviews, and all the personal stories that I had collected. But I didn't. I just thanked him for being honest and wrapped up the call.

It wasn't the only negative feedback I had received, but it was the strongest. And of course, The Impostor sought to pounce on that idea. "What if he's right? What if all those other people were just being nice to you? What if you've done all this work and spent all this time, and no one buys it? You're about to get vulnerable *in print* and tell people all about your insecurities and self-doubt, and all they're going to do is laugh at you!"

Even after all the other positive feedback I'd received, it would have been easy to focus on that one negative comment. Fortunately, it was near the end of my writing process, and I was up to my neck in this book you've been reading.

I had all the tools I needed to recognize the voice of The Impostor and shut it down.

You may be wondering why, after all of my experience and all this study on the subject of impostor syndrome, I would still struggle with The Impostor at all. Why isn't it gone for good?

The answer is simple. This is my first book. Once again, I'm doing (and learning) something new. Every time I attempt something for the first time, The Impostor has an opening to creep back in. I may have completely overcome it in one area, but now there's a fresh, new field for it to plant those seeds of doubt.

Overcoming The Impostor Is a Practice

Freeing yourself from the influence of The Impostor is not a one-time event; it's an ongoing effort. You have to change the way you think, make some conscious decisions that are not natural or comfortable, and step forward at times when you want to step back.

If you act like a Tour Guide, staying in your comfort zone and making the same loop over and over again, The Impostor will usually leave you alone. That's one way to deal with it. You'll build confidence that is based on familiarity and repetition, but you won't do much learning and growing.

On the other hand, if you decide to be an Explorer, you're often going to find yourself in new territory, unfamiliar places where the risk of failure is high. You're going to open up doors for The Impostor and have to deal with it on a regular basis.

The good news is that the effort can, over time, become a set of habits. Like most good habits, they may not be natural at first, but eventually, they can become second nature—an instinctive response.

First, Change the Way You Think

The first set of habits is comprised of changes in your thoughts. These are the internal shifts that take you from thinking like a Tour Guide to an Explorer.

Identify the presence of The Impostor as a good sign. It means that you're pushing yourself outside your comfort zone. The places and moments where The Impostor speaks up are usually the opportunities for growth, learning, and accomplishment. Lean in to those opportunities. Put yourself among people who intimidate you, and benefit from spending time with them. (See chapter 5.)

Remember that failure is not the opposite of success—failure is part of success. It's one of the steps in the process of finding success. Failure never feels good when it happens, but if you walk away from your goal to avoid that feeling, your chances of success go to zero. Don't let failure—even repeated failure—slow you down. Be an Explorer, not a Tour Guide. Know that every person who has ever succeeded at anything has had to push through failure to get there. (See chapter 7.)

Recognize that the ability to learn as you go—to figure out something on the fly while doing it—is a strength, not a weakness. Learning and doing are not mutually exclusive. You can do both at the same time, and that's part of what makes you great. Don't back away from a situation just because you're not 100 percent prepared for it, and don't allow The Impostor to tell you that you're faking it just because you're learning in the process. (See chapters 1 and 5.)

Avoid the trap of comparing yourself and your success to others. You will never really know the truth about another person's story, so measuring the reality of your own life against a filtered and polished version of another life is foolish and dangerous. You should remain focused on your progress, your passions, and most importantly, your purpose. Live your own life, not another person's. (See chapter 8.)

Trust the people who believe in you. When people give you opportunities you don't feel you deserve or challenge you to do things you don't think you're capable of doing, grab hold of those moments, and ride the wave of their confidence. Those are not signs you are a fraud. They're quite the opposite—signs that you don't yet realize what you're capable of. Thankfully, others do. Be grateful for them! (See chapter 1.)

Next, Change the Way You Act and React

The second set of habits are actions, things that you have to practice. They're all centered around the combined power of community and vulnerability.

Accept the compliments that people give you. Don't deflect, don't downplay, and don't allow yourself to rationalize those compliments away in your own head. Receive the praise for the gift that it is, and don't insult the giver. Allow it to build your confidence, and allow yourself to enjoy it. (See chapter 8.)

Say "I don't know." Get comfortable with that phrase. Practice beginning sentences with it any time you really don't have the answer. Share opinions, theories, and ideas as just what they are, without the pretense of expertise. Be honest about the areas where you're learning, and be confident in that learning process. (See chapter 8.)

Find the right mentors, peers, and mentees to create a well-rounded community that will keep you both humble and confident. Manage those relationships like the valuable assets they are. Always be looking for the right people to be in those circles. (See chapter 9.)

Be open and vulnerable, remembering that vulnerability is the key to making your community work for you. Vulnerability is the thing that The Impostor wants you to fear, but it's exactly what you need. Community without vulnerability will feed The Impostor, but community with vulnerability will starve The Impostor. (See chapter 6.)

Share your real story with the people who look up to you. Not the positive spin version that you use when you're in selling mode, but the full story—pros and cons, strengths and weaknesses, triumphs and struggles. Extend hope to others by letting them see that your success has been built on moments of failure, insecurity, and fear, but that those don't define you. (See chapter 6.)

Overcoming The Impostor Begins with One Step

One of my executive coaches once said to me, "The problem with New Year's Resolutions is the 's' at the end. People try to change too many things at once. They should just start with one."

I've given you ten habits—five changes in the way you think and five changes in the way you act and react—that will help you overcome The Impostor. But I know that if you try to master all ten of those changes at once, your chances of success will be low.

But you can start with one change, one step in the right direction. And if you make that step over and over again, it will become a habit. Then you can tackle another. And another.

Choose one now, and for the next thirty days, focus on building that habit. Create a reminder for yourself to review that habit every day, and carefully watch for the opportunities throughout the day to think and act differently.

After a month, or whenever you feel like that habit is part of your natural behavior, choose another one. Review the related chapter from the book, and focus on building that new habit for a while. Recognize how often you have to make a choice to believe or act in a way that feeds The Impostor or in a way that starves it.

Choosing to Lead with Vulnerability

Several years ago, I was invited to join a new peer group of CEOs. We were going to meet once a month to study, learn, and grow together as business leaders. Having been a part of these types of groups in the past, I had learned the importance of vulnerability in making them work.

The combined value of the time of so many executives sitting together for several hours can easily be wasted. If everyone is filtering, only presenting the best version of themselves and their businesses, then learning, growing, and problem solving will be limited. And it can take months, if not years, to build the trust that is needed for people to feel really comfortable opening up to one another.

Most people in the room only knew one or two others, so we started by introducing ourselves and giving a little bit of our background, and I volunteered to go first. I gave a quick overview of my entrepreneurial journey and then dove right in to talking about my battle with The Impostor. I told them how I'd struggled with feeling inadequate because of my lack of a college education and that I'd just been figuring it out for most of my career.

I knew it was a risk. Talking about fears and insecurities with so many strangers was far from comfortable, but I believed that if this group was going to be a good use of my time, we had to get to a place of honesty. And if that level of vulnerability wasn't going to be received well, I'd know this group wasn't for me.

Not only were the other CEOs encouraging, but several others opened up about their struggles and insecurities too. By being vulnerable, I had signaled to everyone that I believed this was a safe place to be real and honest. It accelerated the trust building and set the stage for a productive and insightful day.

At the end of our time together, we were reviewing what we'd learned and giving feedback on the day. One of the CEOs spoke up and said, "I'd like to thank Kris for setting the tone for the day when he shared his background. His willingness to be vulnerable made a big difference. I wasn't sure if this was going to be worth my time, but it was absolutely worthwhile."

Others quickly agreed. No one seemed to view me as weak for opening up and being honest; they saw me as strong. They saw me as a leader among leaders for being willing to do that.

Not everyone will respond to vulnerability with respect the way those executives did. There are definitely people who will shame and punish vulnerability. But I've learned that when that happens, it's also valuable to me because it lets me know exactly what kind of people I'm dealing with. Being vulnerable is a win-win situation. It either builds trust with the people who can handle it, or it exposes those who can't.

Provoking the Change

When I started my first business and someone called me an expert on my third day, I put a lot of pressure on myself to live up to that label. I had a hard time saying "I don't know" because I thought that not having the answer would make me a disappointment, and possibly even a failure, in the eyes of the people around me.

Today, I'm much more comfortable with letting people know where my expertise begins and ends. There are still situations where people assume that I know a lot more than I do, but rather than just letting them go on believing that, I'm getting better at calling that out when I recognize it. I'm willing to dive in and learn, but I don't bother with the pretense of already being an expert.

But as I've studied impostor syndrome for the past several years, I've not only seen a change in myself; I've been able to create change in the people around me. Whether it's speaking to a large audience, setting the tone for a meeting, or coaching an individual who is stressed out and struggling, I have used my story—the real version of my story—to change people's perspectives and to offer them hope.

Every mistake I've ever made, every fear I've ever had, and all the times that I've let The Impostor lie to me are now tools in my tool belt that I can use to help others.

You have many of those same tools; you just need to start using them. You need to connect the dots between those struggles and the powerful lessons that come from them.

The Learning Map

I've developed an exercise that I call "The Learning Map." It will help you to think differently about success, failure, and learning while doing. It's not something to try to rush through quickly. It's going to require some concentration.

Set aside a few hours, and get away from your day-to-day life and work. Take a sheet of paper, and make three columns. You might need more than one sheet before you're finished.

In the left column, make a list of your failures: businesses that went under, projects that didn't succeed, and deals you couldn't close. Include big ones and small ones, and include things that others saw, as well as those things you tried on your own and never let anyone else know about.

Don't hold back, and don't sugar-coat them. This list is for you only, so be real and honest with yourself. List everything you have tried that disappointed you.

In the far right column, make a list of your successes. Again, include big ones and small ones, everything from a product you created to a conversation in which you helped someone solve a problem. Think of as many things as you can, and don't downplay anything. If you're happy with what you did, write it down, no matter how little it may matter to someone else. Again, this is for your eyes only.

In the center column, list the things you have learned. First, look at the failures you've experienced, and list the things you've learned from those failures. Then, look at your successes, and think about what you had to learn to be able to have those successes.

Now, start to connect the items to one another. Draw a line from a failure to a learning to a success. Some of the lines will be straightforward, while others might be more complex: failure > learning > failure > learning > success > learning > success.

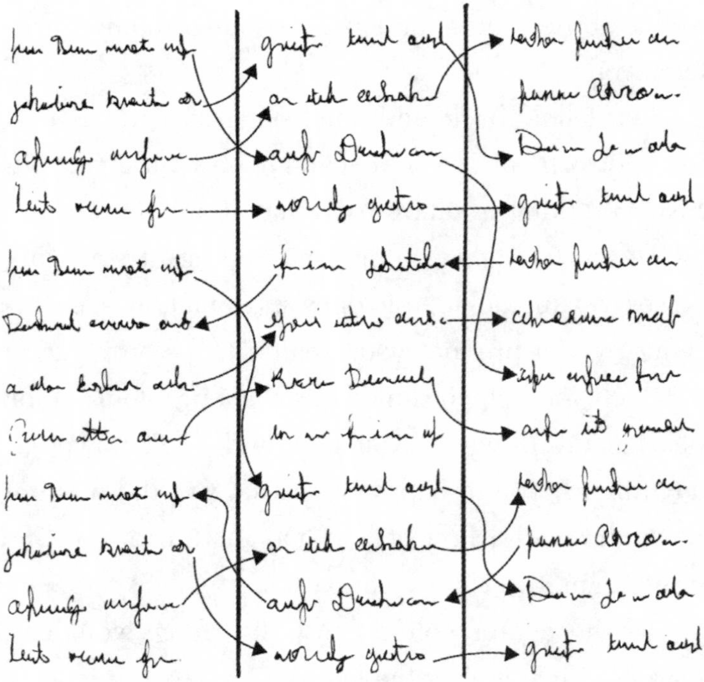

If, in the process of connecting these things you remember another failure, learning, or success, add it to the list. Keep building and connecting until you have a diagram that shows the progress of your career. It may be messy, but that's real life! Life and learning are not straight-line processes.

When you feel you've connected everything there is to connect, take a few moments to look over that list and recognize the value of every failure that has led to learning and success.

This is your story! This is the real truth about your professional journey up to this point. But that story isn't over. It's still being written.

What if you have failures and learnings that don't connect to a success? Well, there's where your opportunities are! What can you do with that valuable experience? Who else might benefit from that experience? How can you turn that into a success for yourself or for someone else?

Now, make one more list. What are the things you would love to do but have been afraid to try because of the possibility of failure? Maybe you'd like to be a public speaker, or you want to start a business or write a book. Maybe you have an artistic side that you've never explored. Maybe you're great at your job, but you'd love to teach. Or maybe you're a teacher, but you'd love to be doing what you see your students going on to do.

That list—the list of potential failures—is actually a list of future learnings and successes. You just can't see them yet. You're an Explorer, and you've identified some unexplored lands. There's a lot of opportunity there, if you are willing to make the journey.

Now, Go Fight the Other Half of the Battle

When I met Jake, he was running a $1 million business with a dozen employees. They did great work and had a stable client base, but Jake wasn't confident that their success would continue.

"I think I may have taken this company as far as I can," he told me. "I wonder if I should step aside and hire a real CEO to take over and grow this business." It was clear that The Impostor was working hard on him.

I convinced Jake to hold off on replacing himself and instead to spend a year working with me as his coach and to meet monthly with a peer group of other business owners. We started working intentionally on the areas that he felt were weak—finances, leadership, communication, and conflict management.

His peer group helped him make some important strategic decisions in hiring the right people, identifying his ideal customer, and eliminating distractions from his core business.

A year later, his revenue had nearly doubled, pushing $2 million. More importantly, he was beginning to lead with confidence. Opening up to his peer group helped him to realize that being a leader is a journey, not a destination, and they were all on that same journey.

Today, Jake has fully embraced his role as CEO of his company. He's getting more and more out of the day-to-day work and being the leader that his employees need him to be. Other leaders among his staff are stepping up as well, following his example.

I told you in chapter 1 that knowing is half the battle (thank you, Saturday morning cartoons). Now you know all about The Impostor and how it tries to trip you up, slow you down, and put artificial limits on everything you do. You also know that it's not really real; it's all in your head.

But don't let the second half of that battle go unfought. Awareness is great, but you have to take action to finish the job. Develop the ten habits. Build your community. Be intentionally vulnerable. And most of all, help others recognize and win their own battle with The Impostor.

You are not an Impostor. You are an Explorer. Explore with confidence!

Things to Consider

Before you go, take a few minutes to think about and answer these questions.

- I listed ten habits (five thoughts and five actions) that can help you to overcome The Impostor. Which one do you most need to build as a practice in your life? What is the first step to creating that habit for yourself?
- It's so valuable to have a group of peers—people who are on a similar journey to yours—with whom you can be vulnerable and authentic. Think of three to five people who you're going

to talk to about your battle with The Impostor. How will you describe it to them?

- Who do you know who seems to be struggling with The Impostor and might benefit from hearing your real story, both the good and the bad, the successes and failures?

ACKNOWLEDGMENTS

First of all, thank you to the hundreds of people who contributed to this book in one way or another. Some of you are my clients, others are friends, and many of you are entrepreneurs I've met over the last fourteen years. Thank you so much for your willingness to be vulnerable and to let me travel with you for part of your journey.

Thank you, Matt West and the entire team at Dexterity. You saw the potential in this book when it was just a simple idea, and you latched on to it and would not let go. Thanks for being patient with me as I learned what it means to author a book. I'm so glad to be part of the Dexterity family.

Thank you, Matt Litton, for the coaching, the ideas, and all the encouragement. This book is easily ten times better than it would have been without your involvement. You are the real deal, and I'll tell anyone who is looking for a writing coach or collaborator that you are the man.

Thank you, Brett Blair! Your help in compiling research, conducting interviews, and brainstorming ideas was such a valuable contribution to this book. It turned out a lot different than we planned it, but I'm so glad to have had you involved, my friend.

Thank you, Jim Cumbee. A lot of people have told me that I should write a book, but you didn't just suggest it; you insisted on it. Your pushing, prodding, reminding, and challenging over the years meant a lot to me. Thank you for caring enough to push.

Thank you, Tom Hill and Roger Hall. The two of you have left a permanent imprint on my life and career, and I'll always be grateful to know you as mentors and as friends.

Thank you, Michael Powers, Allen Jenkins, Tim Altman, Mark Sherrif, Jason Crockarel, Bill Gruenwald, and Will Tenpenny. The time I have spent with you men has been invested wisely. Thank you for your prayers, your wisdom, and your support.

Thank you, Dick Wallace and David Jones. You challenged and encouraged me to overcome The

Impostor before I even recognized it. Thank you for investing your lives in people like me.

Thank you, Rick Lundgren and Hunter Atkins. It's an honor to work alongside the two of you and a privilege to glean wisdom from your experience.

Thank you to all the members (past and present) of my TAB board. I have learned so much from watching you and your businesses grow and mature, and from the advice you offer to me and one another.

Thank you, Vic Gatto, for inviting me to be a part of Jumpstart Foundry. I still mark our first conversation as a pivotal moment in my career. Every time we talk, I leave a little smarter.

Thank you to the entire team at the Nashville Entrepreneur Center for allowing me to teach while I am still learning and to mentor while I am still on the journey.

Thank you, Mike Wharton and John Levy, for doing what great bosses do. You saw things in me that I didn't see in myself and took risks to make that potential a reality. I am very grateful.

Thank you, Mary, my beautiful wife, for believing in me no matter what. You have always seen the very best in me and pushed me to see it too. I would not be the man that I am without you.

Thank You, God, for sending your Son, and for loving me enough to give me a purpose. Thank You for exposing the lies that The Impostor tells me and for opening my eyes to see the truth. And thank You for surrounding me with such incredible people. I love You.

BIBLIOGRAPHY

Books

Christensen, Clayton M. *How Will You Measure Your Life?* New York: Harper Business, 2012.

Collins, Jim. *How the Mighty Fall: And Why Some Companies Never Give In (Good to Great)*. New York: CollinsBusiness Essentials, 2009.

Dweck, Carol S. *Mindset: The New Psychology of Success*. New York: Ballantine, 2007.

Goins, Jeff. *You Are a Writer (So Start Acting Like One)*. Tribe Press, 2014.

Lencioni, Patrick. *The Five Dysfunctions of a Team: A Leadership Fable*. San Francisco: Jossey-Bass, 2002.

Sanders, Tim. *Love Is the Killer App: How to Win Business and Influence Friends*. New York: Currency, 2003.

Websites

Brigham Young University. "Impostor Syndrome Is More Common Than You Think; Study Finds Best Way to Cope with It." ScienceDaily. September 24, 2019. www.sciencedaily.com/releases/2019/09/190924080016.htm

Articles

Fraenza, Christy B. "The Role of Social Influence in Anxiety and the Imposter Phenomenon." *Online Learning* 20, no. 2 (June 2016): http://dx.doi.org/10.24059/olj.v20i2.618.

Hoang, Queena. "The Impostor Phenomenon: Overcoming Internalized Barriers and Recognizing Achievements." *The Vermont Connection* 34, no. 1 (2015): Article 6.

Lane, Joel A. "The Imposter Phenomenon among Emerging Adults Transitioning Into Professional Life: Developing a Grounded Theory." *AdultSpan Journal* 14, no. 2 (2015): 114–28.

Mak, Karina K.L., Sabina Kleitman, and Maree J. Abbott. "Impostor Phenomenon Measurement Scales: A Systematic Review." *Frontiers in*

Psychology 10 (2019): https://doi.org/10.3389/fpsyg.2019.00671.

McGregor, Loretta Neal, Damon E. Gee, and K. Elizabeth Posey. "I Feel Like a Fraud and It Depresses Me: The Relation between the Impostor Phenomenon and Depression." *Social Behavior and Personality* 36, no. 1 (2008): 43–48.

O'Brien McElwee, Rory, and Tricia J. Yurak. "The Phenomenology of the Impostor Phenomenon." *Individual Differences Research* 8, no. 3 (2010): 184–97.

Persky, Adam M. "Intellectual Self-doubt and How to Get Out of It." *American Journal of Pharmaceutical Education* 82, no. 2 (2018): Article 6990.

Sakulku, Jaruwan, and James Alexander. "The Impostor Phenomenon." *International Journal of Behavorial Sciences* 6, no. 1 (2011): 75–97, https://so06.tci-thaijo.org/index.php/IJBS/article/view/521/pdf.

Vergauwe, Jasmine, Bart Wille, Marjolein Feys, Filip De Fruyt, and Frederik Anseel. "Fear of Being Exposed: The Trait-Relatedness of the Impostor Phenomenon and its Relevance in the Work Context." *Journal of Business and Psychology* 30 (2015): 565–81.

NOTES

1. "Impostor syndrome," Wikipedia, last modified October 16, 2020, https://en.wikipedia.org/wiki/Impostor_syndrome.
2. Jane C. Royse Roskowki, "Impostor Phenomenon and Counselling Self-Efficacy: The Impact of Impostor Feelings," Ball State University, 2010.
3. J. Sakulku, "The Impostor Phenomenon," *The Journal of Behavioral Science* 6, no. 1 (September 2011): 75–97. https://doi.org/10.14456/ijbs.2011.6.
4. Adam Savage's Tested, "'Do You Ever Feel Imposter Syndrome?' Adam Q&A (4/28/20)," YouTube video, 40:32, May 3, 2020, www.youtube.com/watch?v=7COvFaFTAy4.
5. Jessica Bruder, "The Psychological Price of Entrepreneurship," *Inc.*, October 16, 2020, www.inc.com/magazine/201309/jessica-bruder/psychological-price-of-entrepreneurship.html.
6. Jeff Haden, "Shark Tank's Barbara Corcoran Says Every Exceptional Person Suffers from Self-Doubt: How to Use Imposter Syndrome to Your Advantage, *Inc.*, March 13, 2020, www.inc.com/jeff-haden/shark-tanks-barbara-corcoran-says-every-exceptional-person-suffers-from-self-doubt-how-you-can-use-imposter-syndrome-to-your-advantage.html.

7. D.E. Hamachek, "Psychodynamics of Normal and Neurotic Perfectionism," Psychology: A Journal of Human Behavior 15, no. 1 (1978): 27–33. https://psycnet.apa.org/record/1979-08598-001.
8. Michael Hyatt, "3 Ways to Go Further, Faster," Michael Hyatt & Co., October 6, 2017, https://michaelhyatt.com/3-ways-to-go-further-faster/.

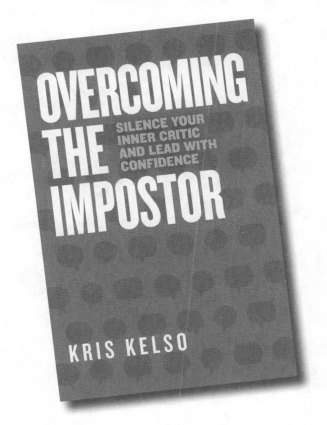